THE OFFICIAL
HANDBOOK OF THE
VAST
RIGHT-WING
CONSPIRACY

MARK W. SMITH

Since 1947
REGNERY
PUBLISHING, INC.
An Eagle Publishing Company • Washington, DC

Copyright © 2008 by Mark W. Smith

All rights reserved. No part of this publication may be reproduced or transmitted in any form or by any means electronic or mechanical, including photocopy, recording, or any information storage and retrieval system now known or to be invented, without permission in writing from the publisher, except by a reviewer who wishes to quote brief passages in connection with a review written for inclusion in a magazine, newspaper, or broadcast.

Library of Congress Cataloging-in-Publication Data

Smith, Mark W., 1968–

   The official handbook of the vast right-wing conspiracy /
   Mark W. Smith
      p. cm.
   Includes bibliographical references.
      ISBN 978-1-59698-049-5
   1. Conservatism—United States. 2. Right and left (Political
science) I. Title.
      JC573.2.U6S644 2008
      320.520973—dc22

                                             2007046450

ISBN 978-1-59698-049-5

Published in the United States by
Regnery Publishing, Inc.
One Massachusetts Avenue, NW
Washington, DC 20001
www.regnery.com

Manufactured in the United States of America

10 9 8 7 6 5 4 3 2 1

Books are available in quantity for promotional or premium use. Write to Director of Special Sales, Regnery Publishing, Inc., One Massachusetts Avenue NW, Washington, DC 20001, for information on discounts and terms or call (202) 216-0600.

Every good faith effort has been made in this work to credit sources and comply with the fairness doctrine on quotation and use of research material. If any copyrighted material has been inadvertently used in this work without proper credit being given in one manner or another, please notify the publisher in writing so that future printings of this work may be corrected accordingly.

The Smoking Gun

The Vast Right-Wing Conspiracy Finally Revealed!

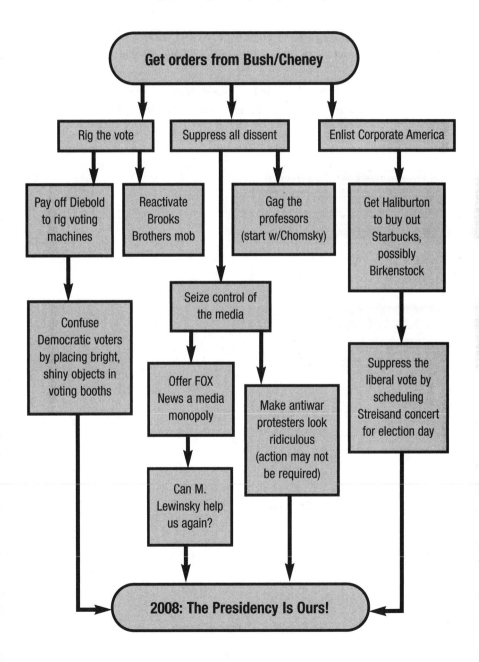

This book is dedicated to the
2007 Nobel Peace Prize winner, Al Gore.

Al, since you won your prize, many liberals have
encouraged you to enter the 2008 presidential race.

On behalf of the Vast Right-Wing Conspiracy,
I also urge you enter the race—so we can beat you again.

CONTENTS

INTRODUCTION

These are trying times for conservatives. In the last few years, we've encountered our share of disappointments: immigration lawlessness, an unending rise in government spending, setbacks in the War in Iraq, and apathy toward the War on Terror are just a few of the challenges we have faced. Even "victories" like the Bush tax cuts now seem uncertain, liable to expire under a tax-addicted Democratic Congress. What's more, the complicity of high-profile Republicans and even the Bush administration itself in many of these problems has demoralized conservatives. It's enough to drive many of us to despair.

★ ★ ★ ★ ★

The mainstream media, of course, finds the situation delightful. It hopes the modern conservative movement that brought us the Reagan revolution, the Contract with America, and the longest peacetime economic expansion in American history has finally been relegated to history's dustbin. The MoveOn.org Left, with its agenda of higher taxes, activist courts, environmental radicalism, and a soft-on-terror foreign policy, is finding plenty of friendly media outlets to disseminate its message—the *New York Times* even gave MoveOn.org a 50 percent discount on an ad attacking the commander of our forces in Iraq, General Petraeus, as a traitor. Helped by the sympathetic mainstream media, Democratic presidential candidates are raising more money than are Republicans, and polls show the public is likely to re-elect a Democrat-controlled Congress.

The question, then, is this: Is the conservative movement finished?

And the answer, of course, is no—not by a long-shot.

Bear in mind Winston Churchill's exhortation to Britons during World War II: "These are not dark days; these are great days—the greatest days our country has ever lived; and we must all thank God that we have been allowed, each of us according to our stations, to play a part in making these days memorable in the history of our race."

Churchill's remarks should put the current moment in perspective for conservatives. Our situation is not nearly as dire as it seems. Despite all the difficulties we face in the War on Terror, we can't ignore our many accomplishments. We overthrew the Taliban in Afghanistan, where Osama bin Laden, if he's still alive, is living in a cave like Fred Flintstone. We deposed Saddam Hussein, one of the worst tyrants of our day. We scared Libya into giving up its WMD program. There's more work to be done, but this is a good start. As demonstrated by World War II and the Cold War, America is a country that faces down worldwide threats—and wins.

You think it's tough being a conservative today? Imagine what it was like for conservatives in the era of Rockefeller Republicans in the late 1960s and early 1970s. The "conservative" choice for president back then was Richard Nixon—the man who went on to introduce racial quotas in federal government contracting, create the Environmental Protection Agency, and appoint the author of *Roe v. Wade*, Harry Blackmun, to the U.S. Supreme Court. At the time, conservatives had hardly any means to communicate their point of view. The mainstream media was liberal, and there was no FOX News Channel, no Internet, and certainly no Sean Hannity, Rush Limbaugh, or Ann Coulter.

Just look at the hurdles Ronald Reagan had to overcome. He became the Great Communicator without any of the "new media" that conservatives rely on today. From the beginning of his presidency, Reagan faced a hostile press and an overwhelmingly Democratic Congress that resisted his policies. And yet, through sheer force of will and his infectious optimism about America, he rammed through a transformative foreign policy based on "peace through strength" that fatally weakened the Soviet Union. At the same time, he saved the American economy from the malaise brought on by peanut farmer extraordinaire Jimmy Carter. Not bad for a guy whose only real advantage over his political opponents was that he had better ideas.

Well, conservatives still have better ideas than liberals, and unlike the Reagan or Nixon eras, now we have the means to communicate them to the public. What I'm saying is that there's no cause for despair—and no time for it. We're facing a crucial presidential election in 2008. Think about what we're likely to face under four, or perhaps eight, years of a Democratic presidency: higher taxes, economic recession, amnesty for illegal aliens, socialized medicine, full retreat in the War on Terror, and much more.

Conservatives considering sitting out this election should consider this: the Supreme Court is evenly divided between four liberal and four conservative justices, with Justice Kennedy casting the swing vote. If a single liberal justice retired and were replaced by a conservative, we would likely secure a conservative majority on the Court for the next twenty years. John Paul Stevens, a liberal Justice, is eighty-seven years old. Draw your own conclusions.

History will show that the current difficult moment is not the end of conservatism, but a slight downturn in a long conservative renaissance that began with the Reagan revolution. Since the Reagan era, we have survived other tough times. Remember that Reagan's successor, George H. W. Bush, violated his "no new taxes" pledge. The resulting demoralization among conservatives led to another blow—the election of Bill Clinton as president. Yet his wife's proposal for "Hillary-care," an outrageous, overreaching attempt to socialize medicine, served as a rallying cry that helped usher in the Gingrich revolution of 1994, when Republicans gained control of both houses of Congress for the first time in forty years.

Since then, conservative values have become so widespread that even the most high-profile liberals have been forced to back away from some of their key positions. President Clinton declared the era of big government to be over and agreed to conservative demands for welfare reform. As a presidential candidate, John Kerry had to mask his poor record on gun rights by pretending to be a hunter. Howard Dean claims that he wants abortion to become "rare."

This edition of *The Official Handbook of the Vast Right-Wing Conspiracy* is part of this conservative renaissance. Our ascent will continue so long as conservatives remain faithful to our core agenda: low taxes, small government, strong national defense, and family values. This is our enduring message. The Republican Party has moved away from this agenda in recent years, and has suffered accordingly. The secret to electoral success is really no secret at all: run as a conservative, govern as a conservative, and voters will reward you. That's what Reagan showed us.

The *Handbook* has been thoroughly revised and updated to provide conservatives with the critical information they need to win arguments for conservatism and American liberty as we head into the 2008 elections. It provides conservatives with the facts and history needed to explain why conservatives are right (pardon the pun) on the issues and why liberals are, well, liberal. The *Handbook* provides sufficient ammunition to help conservatives dispel the oft-repeated myths perpetrated by the Left in its never-ending quest to expand the size and influence of government while subverting traditional American values.

The chapters were determined by the results of a survey conducted by the conservative weekly *Human Events*—the ten issues included herein are the issues conservatives identified as the most important. The book begins with the number one issue—immigration—and presents them, in order, through number ten. It sets out the misguided liberal positions on these topics followed by conservative rebuttals. The *Handbook*, of course, is designed for my fellow members of the Vast Right-Wing Conspiracy. But liberals taking time out from their yoga class to spy on the opposition are also welcome here. Relax, my sprout-eating liberal friends, and read through our program. Who knows what might happen—if you cut your hair, lose the nose ring, and get a job, we might even welcome you into the conspiracy.

ILLEGAL IMMIGRATION: KILLING AMNESTY UNTIL IT'S DEAD

Call it "comprehensive reform," call it a "pathway to citizenship," call it whatever you want—the American people know amnesty when they see it. As they say in Texas, "You can put lipstick on a pig, but you still won't want to kiss it." And the only kiss Americans want to give the open borders crowd is a short kiss goodbye. Open borders politicians tried twice in 2007 to ram amnesty down our throats, and both times Americans rose up in protest and helped to defeat the bills. We have one, simple message for the politicians in Washington: SECURE OUR BORDERS.

★ ★ ★ ★ ★

LIBERAL LUNACY:
"Earned citizenship and guest worker programs are not amnesty."

In 2007, the Senate tried twice to solve the illegal immigration problem through a combination of an "earned citizenship" program for illegals already in America and a "guest worker" program for new immigrants. Unfortunately, a good number of Republicans signed on to this claptrap. Both Senator John McCain—through his immigration proposal sponsored with the Senate's *numero uno* liberal, Ted Kennedy—and President Bush supported this scheme. No matter what they call it, these plans are all tantamount to amnesty.

Back in 1986, we amnestied around 3 million illegal immigrants. The amnesty was sold to us as a one-time deal that would end illegal immigration by legalizing the illegals already here while providing for real immigration enforcement, especially the strict enforcement of the law against employers who hire illegals. But it was a bait-and-switch ploy. The illegals were amnestied, but the enforcement measures never materialized. The result: a tidal wave of illegal immigration over our southern border, resulting in around 12 million illegals in America today.[1] This, of course, is just an estimate—a 2007 study calculated up to 38 million illegals.[2] According to Border Patrol interviews with illegal immigrants, even more illegals attempt to enter the U.S. when they hear that the president is backing a new amnesty proposal.[3]

Americans typically don't fall for the same trick twice. As a result, amnesty supporters now deny that the amnesty they're advocating is an amnesty at all. Because illegals are being asked to fulfill a few conditions like paying a meaningless fine or working for several years under a temporary worker visa before they are granted citizenship, we are told that it's not amnesty—it's "earned citizenship." Well, the bottom line is the same—people who broke our laws and snuck into the country will be rewarded with citizenship.

The attempts at "comprehensive immigration reform" further call for hundreds of thousands of poorly educated workers to enter the country every year under a "guest worker" program. This should really be called a "permanent worker" program, because that's what guest worker programs inevitably become. How did Germany get its large, restive minority of Muslims? They arrived as "guest workers" after World War II and never left. Instead, they brought in their extended families from the Middle East. Rejecting integration, the younger generation of Muslims created a "parallel society" that reflected their native culture.[4]

Let's say we allow in hundreds of thousands of guest workers, and at the end of their terms, they refuse to leave. Then what do we do? Round them up and deport them? Liberals would scream "fascism," just as they do now at anyone who supports the deportation of illegals. If liberals don't support deporting illegals now, why should we believe liberals will support deporting them in the future?

To make their amnesty more palatable, open-borders advocates promise real immigration enforcement at the border and against employers—just like they promised in 1986. With the 1986 amnesty, this crowd demonstrated that it is not serious about enforcement. That's why any solution to the illegal immigration problem must *begin* with enforcement. Once the border is secure and employers can no longer employ illegals with impunity, then we can begin discussing what to do about the illegals already in America.

LIBERAL LUNACY:
"We need an amnesty because there's no practical way to remove 12 million illegal aliens."

Advocates of open borders like to present the solution to illegal immigration as a black and white issue—either we send the paddy wagons to round up every illegal immigrant, or we bow to reality and approve an amnesty.

National Review's John Derbyshire has written about the strange reluctance of the open borders crowd to say what it really means.[5] Here's an update on a short glossary he drew up explaining the unique jargon of open borders advocates.

What the open borders crowd says:	What it really means:
migrant	illegal alien
undocumented worker	illegal alien
match employers with willing workers	open borders
flexible labor market	open borders
legalize	amnesty
regularize	amnesty
guest worker program	amnesty
bring out of the shadows	amnesty
comprehensive immigration reform	amnesty
path to citizenship	amnesty
earned citizenship	amnesty
probationary status	amnesty
temporary visa regime	amnesty
immigration overhaul	amnesty

But neither of these measures is necessary. The key to addressing illegal immigration is to enforce laws against those who employ illegals. New laws don't even have to be approved—we just need to make employers respect the ones that are already on the books.

The overwhelming majority of illegals come to America for work. It's easy for them to find a job, since employers know they can hire illegals with virtually no chance of being penalized. Notwithstanding the occasional showpiece raid that sends Ted Kennedy into fits of sputtering apoplexy, there is an understanding at the highest levels of the U.S.

government that these laws should not be enforced. After Americans rejected the McCain-Kennedy amnesty, the Bush administration finally took a first step toward employer enforcement. In August 2007, it announced a program to pressure employers to fire workers identified as illegal by their fraudulent social security numbers. Unsurprisingly, a San Francisco judge blocked the move.[6] What would happen if one day the government actually began cracking down on employers who hire illegals? Once they had a real disincentive to hiring illegals, you can bet employers would stop doing it. And without job opportunities, illegals would lose the biggest incentive they have to stay in America. We can surmise that not every illegal would return home if they couldn't find a job here, but enough would leave to bring the problem down to much more manageable levels.

LIBERAL LUNACY:
"We need a guest worker program because it's impossible to police a 2,000 mile long border."

America can put a man on the moon, and it can simultaneously defeat Imperial Japan and Nazi Germany. But, according to some, controlling immigration is simply beyond our means. We've tried enforcing the border and it hasn't worked, the open-borders crowd says, so we might as well accept reality and allow "migrants" to come here legally as guest workers.

And while we're at it, we might as well just abolish our laws against rape, murder, and every other crime, since crime still occurs despite all our attempts to eliminate it.

Our efforts in recent decades to secure the border have surely proved inadequate. But does this mean that uncontrolled immigration is inevitable? Absolutely not. Right now, not much more than 10,000 agents are tasked with patrolling the entire southern border. Additional agents are periodically slated to be hired, but funding for them is often stymied in Congress. Similarly, President Bush ordered National Guard troops to the border, but limited their role to functions like training, transport, and surveillance, instead of actually apprehending illegal border crossers.[7]

So what would succeed in securing the border? Two things—first, put enough agents on the border actually to do the job. President Bush's newest plan calls for a total of 20,000 enforcement agents on the border by 2009.[8] This is not enough. According to a report by the Congressional Information Reform Caucus, a total of 36,000 National Guard or state militia troops could likely secure the border.[9] Does it sound impossible to muster that many troops? Look at it this way: each state would have to contribute just 720 troops to halt the flood of illegal immigrants.

Secondly, fences have proven to be an effective deterrent—just look at the San Diego border, formerly America's "number one smugglers' corridor," where the smuggling of people and narcotics fell by 90 percent after the construction of a double-layered border fence.[10] But the U.S. government is playing its usual games with border fencing—in October 2006 President Bush signed the Secure Fence Act, providing for the construction of 700 miles of fencing along the Mexican border. The Department of Homeland Security, led by amnesty supporter Michael Chertoff, has already announced that 330 miles of the fence will be a "virtual fence" consisting of radar, cameras, and other technology—in other words, no fence at all. As for the 370 miles of real fencing that Chertoff agreed to build, nearly a year after President Bush signed the bill into law, Chertoff admitted that only eighty-six miles had been constructed.[11] Even this was an exaggeration according to Congressman Duncan Hunter, who reports that just fourteen miles have been built.[12]

The open borders lobby denounces the planned fence as a "Berlin Wall." Of course, there's one small problem with this comparison—the Berlin Wall was designed to keep a captive people from escaping, whereas the U.S.-Mexico border fence is meant to keep people out who have no legal right to enter the country. It's true that a 700-mile fence would likely just move the flow of illegal immigrants to less secure parts of the border—that's why we should build a fence across the entire border. As the old saying goes, good fences make good neighbors.

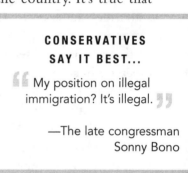

CONSERVATIVES SAY IT BEST...

" My position on illegal immigration? It's illegal. "

—The late congressman Sonny Bono

LIBERAL LUNACY:
"Illegal immigration is not a national security issue because no known terrorists have crossed the border."

Even if we didn't know of any terrorists crossing the border, that wouldn't mean that some group of al Qaeda members hasn't waltzed across the border and is now quietly awaiting orders in some American city. Ever heard of a sleeper cell?

Besides, the supposition that we haven't caught terrorists on the southern border is demonstrably false. In 2006

FBI Director Robert Mueller told a congressional sub-committee that the FBI had busted a Hezbollah smuggling ring that was sending its agents across the Mexican border.[13]

More recently, six Islamic fanatics were arrested in New Jersey while plotting a terrorist attack on the Fort Dix army base. Three of the suspects were illegal immigrants who had accumulated nineteen traffic citations between them. However, because they operated in one of America's many "sanctuary" cities in which the police are largely prevented from reporting illegal immigrants to the federal authorities, the suspects were left free to roam America.[14]

Remember, September 11 also has shown that immigration is a national security issue. At least fifteen of the nineteen hijackers were in America on that fateful day even though they should have been denied visas—if immigration officials had processed their applications properly. And don't forget Ahmed Ressam, the Algerian-born would-be terrorist who was arrested in 1999 trying to cross the Canadian border in order to bomb the Los Angeles airport.[15] According to the Census Bureau, 114,818 Middle Eastern men and women were estimated to be in the U.S. illegally in 2000. Will any of these people ever perpetrate another terrorist attack on American soil? Are you willing to bet your life that none of them ever will?

The Beltway sniper, Lee Malvo, and his mother were illegal immigrants from Jamaica. They were arrested in Bellingham, Washington, in 2001. The arresting officers noted in writing that Malvo and his mother should be imprisoned until deportation charges were resolved. This did not happen. Instead, Malvo, despite being caught as an illegal alien, was released without bond. Shortly after his release, Malvo, with the help of his partner, John Muhammad, went on a killing spree along the Washington Beltway, murdering ten people and causing widespread public panic. What's the use of spending tax dollars to capture illegal aliens if we just release them back onto the streets? Illegal aliens who are captured should be deported. For the sake of our safety, we need stricter immigration enforcement and control.

Make no mistake about it—illegal immigration is a national security issue of the highest priority.

> ### The *Real* Reason for Liberals' Support for Illegal Immigration
>
> " Democrats are counting on illegal immigrants to be the future of their party, their border guards for the new socialist state. At least liberals have a clear mission and know what they're fighting for. Their plan is to destroy America. "
>
> —Ann Coulter[16]

LIBERAL LUNACY:
"Conservatives will lose votes by opposing illegal immigration."

Illegal immigration is an increasingly important problem for the American people. The collection of open border ideologues, multiculturalism zealots, and opportunistic employers who oppose border security are really a small minority.

Too many conservatives buy into the stale liberal rhetoric claiming that voters are turned off by "mean-spirited" campaigns against illegal immigration. The prime example, supposedly, is the decline in the fortunes of the Republican Party in California, which they attribute to the anti-illegal immigration position of former California

Governor Pete Wilson. What liberals and their open-borders allies don't like to mention is that during Wilson's tenure, California voters approved by wide margins three initiatives to fight illegal immigration and to scale back multicultural programs. Making support for Proposition 187—a ballot initiative that called for eliminating some state assistance to illegal immigrants—his primary campaign issue, Wilson won re-election in 1994 by a whopping 15 percentage points. And California voters themselves approved Prop 187, although the bill was effectively killed off by the courts. It was the abandonment of Wilson's anti-illegal immigration platform by his successors in the California GOP leadership that cost the party so dearly at the polls.[17] In fact, a key issue in the recall of former California governor Gray Davis was Davis' approval of a bill to allow illegal aliens to obtain driver's licenses. Arnold Schwarzenegger campaigned against the measure, which surveys showed was opposed by 70 percent of Californians, in his successful run to replace Davis.[18] More recently, New York's Democratic governor, Eliot Spitzer, also advocated drivers licenses for illegals. Even in New York, the bluest of the blue states, the plan provoked a popular uproar, forcing the governor to abandon his plan.[19]

Illegal immigration has already emerged as a key issue in the 2008 elections, as evidenced by its selection as the single most important issue by the respondents to the survey that guided this book. And it is not only conservatives who understand the urgency to begin addressing the problem. In fact, a 2005 Zogby poll found that those most opposed to illegal immigration are Democrats, African Americans, women, and people with a household income under $75,000.[20] Far from being an electoral loser, taking a strong stand against illegal immigration represents an opportunity for conservatives to pick off traditionally Democratic voters.

LIBERAL LUNACY:
"Multiculturalism and diversity are good for our society."

Is that so? So we should emphasize our differences over our similarities? We should encourage immigrants to embrace the culture of the place they abandoned and reject the culture of the place to which they ran? Great idea! Maybe we'll end up like one of those places where ethnic and cultural differences matter more than anything else—say, Northern Ireland or Bosnia, or maybe Rwanda or Darfur. Gee, I can't wait!

Let's face it: multiculturalism is dangerous to our nation. In October and November 2005, Muslim rioters burned businesses, cars, and buildings in France. Though debate exists over the rioters' motives, one thing appears clear: France has failed to assimilate these Muslim youths into the nation's wine and Brie culture. We can only hope American immigrants never feel this way about hamburgers, hot dogs, and barbeque.

However, the sight of massive pro-amnesty demonstrations in April and May 2006, featuring tens of thousands of people waving Mexican flags, calling for a boycott of U.S. businesses, and holding placards rejecting U.S. sovereignty ("America is a continent, not a country," read one sign; "USA = United States of Mexico," read another), should serve as a warning.[21]

Even Bill Clinton saw the danger: "Ethnic pride," he noted in a 1998 speech, "is a very good thing. America is one of the places which most reveres the distinctive ethnic, racial, religious heritage of our various peoples. The days when immigrants felt compelled to Anglicize their last name or deny their heritage are, thankfully, gone. But pride in one's ethnic and racial heritage must never become an excuse to withdraw from the larger American community. That does not honor diversity; it breeds divisiveness. And that could weaken America."[22]

Clinton must have been having one of those "New Democrat" days: He even spoke in favor of having immigrants learn English: "Now, it's all very well for someone to say, every one of them should learn English immediately. But we don't at this time necessarily have people who are trained to teach them English in all those languages. So I say to you, it is important for children to retain their native language. But unless they also learn English, they will never reach their full potential in the United States."[23]

I may never utter these words again, but here goes nothing: Bill Clinton was right. Immigrants should be forced to acclimate themselves to American culture—not vice versa. If they want to come to the U.S., then they have to speak English. We don't want a balkanized America split into warring ethnic or racial groups. We should impress on Americans that there is a unique American identity that is inseparable from the American way of freedom and democracy.

Unfortunately, the U.S. government does not seem to share Clinton's view of the importance of the English language. In April 2007, the Equal Employment Opportunity Commission (EEOC) sued the Salvation Army—one of the nation's most esteemed charities—for firing two employees at one of its thrift stores who refused to learn English. The Salvation Army has an English-only policy at the workplace, and two non-English speaking employees were given a year to learn the language. After a year they had failed, so the Salvation Army let them go. And in jumped the EEOC screaming "discrimination." So much for the importance of English.[24]

We also need to eliminate bilingual education programs. They burden taxpayers while encouraging foreign-language speaking immigrants to refuse to learn English. How does it help immigrants in New York, Chicago, or Los Angeles to give them a chance to speak Farsi, Greek or Spanish—but no incentive to learn English? Forget what's best for the U.S.; how does this help the immigrant get ahead? When an immigrant comes to the U.S., he should be encouraged to become a true American, not a hyphenated American. He should learn English and understand the value of hard work, self-sufficiency and independence.

> **MAINSTREAM MEDIA:**
> **"Mexican flags?**
> **What Mexican flags?"**
>
> " I used to write this sort of press-releasey 'news' account when my college paper assigned me to 'cover' anti-war demonstrations that I'd helped organize! "
>
> —Blogger Mickey Kaus, on the *LA Times'* coverage of the 2006 pro-illegal immigration rallies, in which the paper downplayed the huge number of Mexican flags carried by demonstrators.[25]

LIBERAL LUNACY:
"Illegal immigrants do jobs that Americans don't want to do."

Actually, the more accurate statement is: "Illegal immigrants do jobs that Americans don't want to do at the current wage rates." So what? Without illegal immigrants would fruit and vegetables be rotting in fields? Would there be no nannies for toddlers in yuppie families or a lack of hotel towel launderers? In fact, illegal immigrants are not essential to our economy. If there were a decrease in cheap, illegal immigrant labor, employers would simply have to substitute higher priced domestic employees, legal immigrants, or better technology.

Still, it's true: to deport illegal aliens would cause some disruptions. But not for very long. Employers would make the necessary adjustments. Many tasks would be mechanized. We can use robots to build cars and even to explore Mars. Why can't we employ mechanization to help harvest crops? Professor George J. Boras, an economics professor at Harvard University, points to states like Iowa where foreign-born residents are relatively few, yet there are plenty of Americans working in hotels, fast-food restaurants, and other jobs elsewhere held by illegal immigrants.[26]

Indeed, although liberal journalists living on Manhattan's Upper West Side may fear the prospect of not having illegal immigrants to clean the tables at their French bistros, or to watch the children while Dad goes to work for the *Village Voice* and Mom for Planned Parenthood, the reality is that they could just pay a little more to hire legal help.

LIBERAL LUNACY:
"How we can justify turning our backs on the world's poorest people?"

I am not going to apologize for saying that our elected officials need to worry about America first. Every other country puts its own interests first; why should America be different? If we accepted every immigrant who wanted to move here, there would be hundreds of millions of foreigners here tomorrow—causing untold problems for our national security and economy.

Conservatives should support legal immigration, but not illegal immigration. There is no constitutional or other right for foreigners to immigrate to the U.S.; nevertheless, the U.S. should embrace immigration when doing so advances our national interests. We already have the most generous immigration policy in the world. The U.S. admits roughly 800,000 legal immigrants each year who are eligible to become citizens. This is greater than all nations in Western Europe combined and more than at any point in American history.[27]

And yet, we are constantly lectured by Mexican officials about our supposedly insensitive treatment of illegal immigrants. And how do the Mexicans themselves treat illegal immigrants in their own country? According to the U.S. State Department, in 2006 "there were credible reports that police, immigration, and customs officials frequently violated the rights of undocumented migrants, including rape. Robbery and killings by the criminal gangs, such as the Mara Salvatrucha and Barrio 18, intensified on the southern border and spread northward. Undocumented migrants rarely filed charges in such cases because the authorities generally deported such persons who came to their attention."[28] So illegal immigrants in Mexico get raped by government officials, and they are deported if they report being victimized by gangs. Remember that the next time a Mexican official criticizes "harsh" U.S. immigration policies.

Those who are ready and able to work should be welcomed to America. Immigration has always strengthened the country and benefited the economy. However, we should choose carefully. We don't want immigrants who will cost taxpayers more than they bring to the table. Anyone, of course, is welcome to support immigrants through their own charitable activities. But if an immigrant thinks he is going to get social services paid for by the tax dollars of hardworking Americans, send him home. We don't need to be the welfare system or soup kitchen to the world.

VRWC TALKING POINTS

★ "Comprehensive reform," "earned citizenship," and other "legalization" schemes are all forms of amnesty.

★ Enforcing existing laws against employers who hire illegal immigrants would be a huge help in solving the illegal immigration problem. Mass deportations are not necessary.

★ Illegal immigration is not inevitable across the Mexican border. Building a fence and hiring enough patrolmen to guard it will stem the flow.

★ As shown by September 11, the Beltway snipers, and the Fort Dix jihadists, illegal immigration is a national security issue of the highest priority.

★ The open borders crowd is a small minority opposed by most Americans. Standing against amnesty and supporting border enforcement is a winning position for conservative politicians.

★ Multiculturalism is dangerous for America, while assimilation is the path to success for immigrants.

★ Americans will do the jobs illegal immigrants are now doing—they only need a fair wage.

★ Every nation has the right to control its own borders. Immigrants who contribute to our economy should be welcome; immigrants who come for welfare should not.

THE WAR ON TERROR: APPEASE THIS!

As Islamic terrorists continue their campaign to wipe out the entire non-Muslim world, liberals insist on the need to "understand" their grievances. Note to liberals: we could withdraw our troops from Iraq, use them to attack Israel, and throw President Bush into a cell in Guantanamo Bay. But unless we adopt Islamic sharia law in America, the jihadists will still try to kill us.

$$\star \quad \star \quad \star \quad \star \quad \star$$

LIBERAL LUNACY:
"We don't need terrorist profiling or enemy combatant designations. We can handle terrorism as a law enforcement issue."

When former Democratic senator John Edwards dismissed the War on Terror as a "bumper sticker" slogan, he gave voice to the commonly-held liberal belief that the threat of Islamic terrorism is overstated. We were alerted to the problem on September 11, liberals claim, and now we're on our guard. The terrorists probably won't attack us again, and if they try, we'll surely catch them. So we can stop focusing on these pesky national security problems, and concentrate on things that Americans really care about—important issues like socializing health care and saving the endangered cave snail.

In reality, Islamic terrorists are out to kill us like never before, and they'll continue their efforts until they either succeed or are defeated. And as long as the threat remains, we need to take proactive measures to defend ourselves against it. We simply cannot rely on our usual police procedures or the court system to fight against Islamic fanatics who dedicate their lives to finding ways to kill Americans and destroy Western civilization. That would be a return to a pre-September 11 mindset.

Liberals decry common-sense demands to profile for terrorists at airports. Pretending that terrorists are not highly likely to be young, Middle Eastern men, liberals insist on random searches of passengers, so that eighty-year-old grandmothers are just as likely to be stopped and questioned as is Muhammad Jihad traveling on a one-way ticket with no luggage other than his Koran.

What's more, liberals vehemently insist that terrorism suspects be accorded the same rights as your average petty criminal. They insist on applying the Geneva Conventions to terrorism suspects, even though the Conventions were not meant to apply to independent, stateless terrorist groups. And liberals whine about the "rights" of the dangerous enemy combatants held at Guantanamo Bay, seeking to give them lawyers and bury their cases in a morass of civil litigation; in other words, they want to reward captured foreign terrorists by extending to them the constitutional rights of U.S. citizens.

Here's a news flash: members of stateless terrorist groups like al Qaeda have no rights, either under the Geneva Conventions or under the U.S. Constitution. We should hold them for the duration of the conflict, until it's safe to release them—if ever. The war on Islamic terrorism is a deadly serious business that should be led by the president, not the courts. As *National Review* noted, "The executive makes both the decisions [about] whom to capture and whom to bomb based on determinations that cannot be second-guessed in civilian courts, lest the commander in chief have to argue his every act of war in court."[1]

The discovery in the last few years of numerous terrorist plots in the West shows that we cannot afford to become complacent. Less than two days before he was killed by U.S. soldiers, Taliban commander Mullah Dadullah told ABC News that he was training U.S. and British citizens to carry out suicide terrorist attacks in the U.S. and Britain.[2] Perhaps we should take him at his word.

Can we really afford to treat terrorism like any other crime and give unelected judges the power to micromanage our national defense efforts? The answer is a clear, emphatic "no."

Recent Terror Plots in the West

- In June 2006 a Canadian jihadist cell was busted while planning to seize hostages in the Canadian parliament and behead Prime Minister Stephen Harper.

- In August 2006 British police arrested a jihadist group planning to blow up as many as ten commercial airliners in flight from Britain to the U.S.

- In May 2007 six jihadists were arrested for conspiring to slaughter U.S. soldiers at Fort Dix.

- In June 2007 a jihadist plot to set off massive car bombs in London and Glasgow was narrowly averted.

LIBERAL LUNACY:
"To fight terrorism, we must recognize the root
causes of terror, such as poverty."

A lot of Christians, Jews, Buddhists, and Hindus are poor, unhappy, or didn't get enough hugs when they were kids. But for some reason, they don't react to these disadvantages by declaring holy war on the entire world.

The notion that terrorists are motivated by poverty is not only farcical, but it's demonstrably untrue. Marc Sageman, a forensic psychiatrist and former CIA case officer, studied the biographies of four hundred al Qaeda-linked terrorists. His findings repudiated the myth that terrorism is linked to poverty: "In terms of socio-economic background, three-fourths [of the terrorists studied] come from upper and middle class families. Far from coming from broken families, they grew up in caring intact families, mildly religious and concerned about their communities. In terms of education, over 60 percent have some college education. . . . Most of the terrorists have some occupational skills. Three-fourths are either professional (physicians, lawyers, architects, engineers, or teachers) or semi-professionals (businessmen, craftsmen, or computer specialists). They are solidly anchored in family responsibilities. Three-fourths are married and the majority have children."[3]

These conclusions were most dramatically illustrated in the June 2007 jihadist car bombing plot in Britain, where nearly all the arrested suspects were doctors. When was the last time you met a poor doctor?

If we look at what the terrorists themselves say—from the testimony left by September 11 ringleader Muhammad Atta to the "martyrdom videos" recorded by Palestinian suicide bombers—there is one ever-present theme. And it's not poverty—it's Islam. All the terrorists invoke the Koran and its many verses calling for jihad against infidels. And from where do they derive this interpretation of Islam? It's taught to them, largely through a worldwide program for funding mosques, charities, cultural organizations, and student groups carried out by Saudi Arabia. The Saudis spend obscene amounts of their oil money every year spreading an anti-Western religious ideology—*Wahhabism*—that inculcates its adherents with a poisonous, violent, Islamic supremacist creed. Saudi money not only empowers Wahhabism against less extreme strands of Islam throughout the Arab world, but it also finances the *madrasas* (fundamentalist Islamic schools) in Pakistan and Afghanistan that gave rise to the Taliban.[4]

And if you think Saudi funding of Islamism is not an issue in America, guess again. In 2006, Freedom House published a report on Saudi government-sponsored literature disseminated at U.S. mosques. What the researchers found was the most repugnant, anti-American, anti-Christian, and anti-Semitic hate literature imaginable. The report concluded that the Saudi government was spreading a " 'totalitarian ideology of hatred that can incite to violence,' " and the fact that it is 'being mainstreamed within our borders through the efforts of a foreign government, namely Saudi Arabia, demands our urgent attention.' "[5]

So we can forget about the false notion of poverty turning Muhammad Sixpack into a crazed suicide bomber. If we want to address the root causes of terrorism, we should start by pressing the Saudis to stop their massive, medieval-style campaign of incitement to anti-Western hatred.

According to Freedom House's Report, "Saudi Publications on Hate Ideology Invade American Mosques," Saudi Literature in U.S. Mosques:

- encourages Muslims to hate Christians and Jews

- condemns America and democracy as un-Islamic

- encourages the murder of those who convert from Islam

- demands that Muslims living in non-Islamic countries concentrate on gathering intelligence or making money to be used later in a jihad against the infidels. They may also focus on converting the infidels to Islam

- pronounces it lawful to rob and kill Muslims who don't uphold Wahhabi sexual mores

- advocates that women be veiled, segregated from men, and barred from various jobs

LIBERAL LUNACY:
"9/11 was an inside job."

Our leftist friends have always had an affinity for conspiracy theories, especially those alleging that the evil U.S. government has committed some monstrous atrocity. So perhaps it was inevitable that the most devastating terrorist attack in America's history would come to be blamed on the U.S. itself.

After September 11, the conspiracy theory that the U.S. government had engineered the attacks was largely confined to the Arab world and to the farthest fringes of the American Left. But recently, the canard has become more widespread among American liberals, spawning an entire movement—"the Truthers"—that has become a permanent fixture at leftwing protests.

Liberal stalwart Rosie O'Donnell proclaimed on television that the World Trade Center 7 building, which collapsed after being weakened by falling debris from the North Tower, was really demolished by explosives. Her beliefs are no longer unusual on the Left. According to a May 2007 Rasmussen poll, 35 percent of Democrats believe that President Bush had advance knowledge of the September 11 attacks, while another 26 percent say they are not sure.[6] In other words, over 60 percent of Democrats will not rule out the possibility that September 11 was a government conspiracy. Unsurprisingly, Democratic leaders have begun pandering to their conspiracy-obsessed base; when John Edwards was asked by a conspiracy theorist about the collapse of World Trade Center 7, Edwards amazingly promised the kook that he'd look into the allegations.

The September 11 conspiracy theory took off among liberals after it was detailed in *Loose Change*, a low-budget but slick-looking "documentary" with eerie theme music that sounds like something ripped off from the *X-files*. The film has gone through various permutations, with each edition heavily edited to remove the many errors highlighted by the film's critics. The film's allegations vary dramatically depending on the edition, but the general theory is that the planes that brought down the World Trade Center towers were not passenger airliners, but military planes that fired missiles just before crashing into the buildings, which had been softened up by controlled demolitions of explosives planted in the towers beforehand. The World Trade Center 7 building also supposedly collapsed due to explosives, while the Pentagon was allegedly hit by a cruise missile instead of a plane. As for the crash of Flight 93 in Pennsylvania, the filmmakers initially claimed the plane was shot down by another plane, but in later editions began arguing that it never crashed at all.

It's impossible to disprove the theory to Truthers, because they dismiss every piece of opposing evidence as being tainted by the conspiracy. If you point out that Osama bin Laden admitted on videotape to masterminding the September 11 attacks, they claim that the tape was a forgery manufactured by the U.S. government that featured a bin Laden look-alike. If you note that all the real hijackers died in the September 11 attacks, they argue that this is disinformation, and that many of these people, in fact, are still alive. If you draw attention to the passengers' phone calls to various people on September 11 reporting that their flight had been hijacked, they insist that the government falsified the calls by using super-duper voice-morphing technology.

The laughable theories, supported in the film by supposed experts ranging from the late "gonzo journalist" Hunter S. Thompson to an anonymous caller to the Howard Stern show, were debunked by researchers from the National Institute of Standards and Technology,[7] *Popular Mechanics* magazine,[8] The History Channel,[9] and countless others. But that doesn't prove anything except that they're in on the conspiracy, according to Truthers.

Ultimately, Truthers are never able to answer two questions. First, how is it that the U.S. government is so ruthless and powerful that it can massacre thousands of its own citizens and cover it up, but cannot prevent a couple of guys from releasing a documentary exposing the entire plot? And secondly, how does the Easter Bunny fit into all this?

LIBERAL LUNACY:
"9/11 was caused by America's arrogant foreign policy. America needs to stop angering the 'Arab street.'"

The world toward which the jihadists strive cannot peacefully coexist with the Western world. The Western world is based upon the belief that ordinary people should have the opportunity to make their own life choices for themselves and their families. In stark contrast, militant Islamic leaders want to create a world in which they make the life decisions for their subjects to best advance the views of Allah and Muhammad.

Think of Iran. Iran's current leadership consists of extremely dangerous anti-American and anti-Israel lunatics. Iranian president Mahmoud Ahmadinejad—a former member of Iran's secret police—is a Holocaust denier who demands that Israel be "wiped off the map." Ahmadinejad claims that he felt God helping him during a 2005 speech to the United Nations and also believes in "the Shiite prophecy that the twelfth imam, or the messiah, would return to save the believers and kill the infidels" and that this "would happen in the next two years."[10]

But they only hate us because we support Israel, the Left argues. Well, jihadists would keep trying to destroy the U.S. even if we fed Israel to the wolves tomorrow. Want proof? Consider this: Osama bin Laden didn't say even one word about U.S. policy toward Israel and the Palestinians until after September 11, although he had had plenty to say before then about how evil the West is. The notion that we can somehow appease jihadists by any policy other than turning America into an Islamic country is delusional. Look at the signs held by the radical British Muslims who went berserk after a Danish newspaper published some cartoons satirizing Muhammad. They read: "Behead those who insult Islam" and "Freedom go to hell." Do these sound like people who can be appeased by a change in foreign policy?

Anyway, it wouldn't matter if the U.S. really were the global terrorist state that radical Muslims (along with much of the American Left) likes to pretend it is: No matter how valid any complaints against the U.S. may be, nothing can justify terrorist attacks against innocent, unarmed civilians. Our task is not to sit around and figure out what particular grievance motivated the terrorists to bring down the Twin Towers. The point is that they did it, and now we have to defend ourselves and destroy them. This is war. We must win.

When the jihadists attacked us on September 11, the Blame-America-First crowd, which had been relatively quiet since the collapse of their last "favorite team," the Soviet Union, sprang back into action. Reality check: September 11 was not our fault. It was the direct result not of what the U.S. has done, but of who we are and what we represent. Militant Islamists cannot stomach a tolerant, free society that allows for freedom of religion. We pose a threat to their vision of an Islamic utopia on Earth simply because we do not all bow to Mecca several times a day.

Our free society has made us the envy of the world, as well as the world's preeminent nation militarily, economically, and culturally. But radical Muslims resent our global superiority. They're looking for ways to knock us down a peg. They delight in criticizing our decadence and immorality—although these same Islamic moralists were deafeningly silent about the morality in the rape and torture of Saddam Hussein's prisoners. Nor did they have much to say about the palaces Saddam built with emergency aid money meant for Iraq's civilians.

Let's get something straight: The U.S. is the most generous nation in the world. When the tsunami hit Southeast Asia, Americans donated $1 billion privately, and the U.S. government gave $950 million on top of providing all sorts of other financial, military, and moral support to the victims. Hurricane Katrina? Two and a half billion donated. American taxpayers shell out $6–9 billion in foreign aid each year. Muslim countries get a great deal of this—Egypt alone sucks up over $2 billion a year. And if America didn't buy any oil, Arab states would be even worse off than they are now (and would probably be getting even more billions in American aid).

Meanwhile, U.S. presidents since Jimmy Carter have tried to mediate a just settlement of the Israeli-Palestinian dispute—one that would be fair to both sides (despite the fact that doing so would reward the Palestinians for their terrorist attacks). In 2000, the U.S. elected a president who supports the creation of a Palestinian (i.e., Arab Muslim) state to help resolve the Israel-Palestinian stalemate. In the 1990s, the U.S. helped rescue Muslims in both Bosnia and Kosovo from "ethnic cleansing" by Serbs. Also in the 1990s, the U.S. tried to feed starving Somali Muslims—leading to the "Black Hawk Down" debacle, which claimed the lives of eighteen U.S. soldiers. In the 1980s, the U.S. helped Muslims fighting in Afghanistan against the Soviet Union.

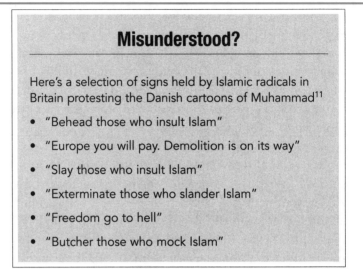

Misunderstood?

Here's a selection of signs held by Islamic radicals in Britain protesting the Danish cartoons of Muhammad[11]

- "Behead those who insult Islam"
- "Europe you will pay. Demolition is on its way"
- "Slay those who insult Islam"
- "Exterminate those who slander Islam"
- "Freedom go to hell"
- "Butcher those who mock Islam"

What did the U.S. get in return for these efforts? We got September 11. Great trade! Weakness, generosity, concessions and appeasement have only emboldened the terrorists. Islamic militants are not moved by our good intentions, earnest efforts, and charity—to them, anyone who is not in the House of Islam must be destroyed.

LIBERAL LUNACY:
"Islam is a religion of peace. It is racist
and wrong to suggest that the terrorists have
anything to do with true Islam."

I smell something. Did someone just bring a red herring in here? Sure, most Muslims aren't terrorists. But it was only militant Islamists who perpetrated and celebrated the mass murder of 3,000 people on September 11. Liberals can walk around telling themselves that this is not a holy war, but the militant Islamists obviously did not get the memo.

There is a good reason for this. These terrorists think they're fighting an Islamic jihad, just as Muslims have done since the seventh century. In the radical Muslim view, Islam is a religion of peace only for those who believe in and follow the Koran—especially parts like what Muslims know as the Verse of the Sword, for which Osama has praised Allah in one of his communiqués. You know the one: it goes, "Slay the unbelievers wherever you find them" (Koran, Sura 9:5).

Renowned Islamic scholar Bernard Lewis explains, "One of the basic tasks bequeathed to Muslims by the Prophet [Muhammad] was jihad." Lewis says that the "overwhelming majority of early authorities, citing the relevant passages of the [Koran], the commentaries, and the traditions of the Prophet, discuss jihad in military terms. According to Islamic law, it is lawful to wage war against . . . infidels [and] apostates" and that such a jihad is "a religious obligation."

That means that Marin County's John Walker Lindh (aka Abdul Hamid), the kid from California who converted to Islam and ended up fighting with the Taliban against U.S. troops, was only doing what he thought Allah wanted him to do. So was Osama himself on September 11. So are the thousands upon thousands of members of Islamic terrorist groups around the world today.

To jihadists, if you're with the program, you're okay. But if not, then you're either an apostate or an infidel and deserve to be killed. As a non-Muslim nation, America can expect about as much peace from the militant Islamists as was given to the huge, ancient Buddha statues in Afghanistan—destroyed by the Taliban in 2001 in the name of Islamic purity.

Bottom line: The U.S. is at war. The threat we face today from militant Islam is no different (except in name and philosophical foundation) than the previous threats we faced from the racial fascism of Nazism and the economic fascism of Communism.

How is it that liberals, who have found in the Constitution—voilà!—unexpressed "individual rights" to abortion, sodomy, and Miranda warnings, suddenly turn a blind eye to the clear nature and motives of the terrorists who are seeking our destruction? We didn't ask for a religious war or a clash of civilizations, but that's just what the radical Muslims are fighting. If we don't defend ourselves, then Heaven help us. (Translation for liberals: "Then Noam Chomsky help us.")

LIBERAL LUNACY:
"President Bush is exaggerating the threat of terrorism to gain political support."

Ted Kennedy said this one. Ted, do you really think President Bush's work to defend the country is one big "fraud"? Do you think those planes flying into the World Trade Center were just Hollywood props? Tell that to any American who lost a loved one on September 11. Tell it to Lisa Beamer and to the child who will never know her heroic father, Todd Beamer, who was killed on United Airlines Flight 93 after storming the hijacked plane's cockpit along with other passengers.

Look into their eyes, Ted. Tell them that avenging the deaths of their loved ones is a fraud. Tell them that fighting to prevent future attacks is a cynical attempt to gain political advantage. What do you think they will say?

Karl Rove got it right by observing, "Perhaps the most important difference between conservatives and liberals can be found in the area of national security. Conservatives saw the savagery of September 11 and the attacks and prepared for war; liberals saw the savagery of the September 11 attacks and wanted to prepare indictments and offer therapy and understanding for our attackers. . . . I don't know about you, but moderation and restraint is not what I felt as I watched the Twin Towers crumble to the earth; a side of the Pentagon destroyed; and almost three thousand of our fellow citizens perish in flames and rubble. Moderation and restraint is not what I felt—and moderation and restraint is not what was called for."[12]

Should we be surprised by the Left's reaction? No. After spending eight years defending the self-indulgent, nihilistic, and military-cutting Clinton administration, liberals may not be able to believe that an American president could be motivated by anything but cynical, calculating self-aggrandizement. They've forgotten that the government's primary purpose is to defend the country (no, Hillary, not to tell us how to live our lives and raise our children). The September 11 attacks, the ceaseless terrorist offensive against Israel (the only Western-style democracy in the Middle East), and the attacks on U.S. soldiers in Iraq make it mind-boggling that anyone would claim that the terrorist threat is exaggerated.

In reality, conservatives understate the threat. Though the terrorists may lack the military, economic, and technological means to destroy the West, their use of modern technology gives them the capacity to inflict catastrophic casualties. Make no mistake: If al Qaeda or any other terrorist organization had had a nuclear weapon on September 11, they would have used it. Then the left-wing talking heads at the *New York Times* wouldn't even be here to question the president's motives.

LIBERAL LUNACY:
"The Patriot Act is unconstitutional and
endangers individual rights."

Name that person! Name the person who has been oppressed or abused by the Patriot Act. Look, if you are dumb enough to check out *The Anarchist Cookbook* from the local library (and you're not writing a thriller novel), then you deserve to be arrested for sheer stupidity. Does the Left really think President Bush is spying on folks who checked out Maya Angelou poems? Shortly after September 11, Congress overwhelmingly passed the Patriot Act. What does the Patriot Act do to help thwart future terrorist attacks in the United States? It eliminates legal barriers that prevent federal intelligence officials from sharing information with law enforcement. Let's go to the videotape. Before September 11, the FBI had captured Zacarias Moussaoui along with his laptop computer. Did someone look at the laptop to see what it contained? No. But why? Because of the concern that doing so might violate the barrier preventing law enforcement officials and federal intelligence agencies from exchanging information with each other—even when they're investigating the same individuals and groups. The Patriot Act put an end to this insanity.

Another benefit of the Patriot Act is that law enforcement officials no longer need to procure a separate warrant for each computer or cell phone a terrorist suspect might use. This simple updating of federal law to catch up with modern wireless and digital technologies should worry no one.

Liberals often scream hysterically about how the Patriot Act might allow government to learn the titles of books you borrow from libraries. Apparently, the Left forget that public libraries are *public* because they are *owned and run by the government.* Thus, the government already knows if you're checking out *The Anarchist Cookbook.* But why would the Left let silly little facts interfere with attacks against a Republican president?

The Patriot Act has been around for years now, so where's all the evidence of these supposed abuses? Did President Bush use the Patriot Act to deploy armed federal agents to rip a six-year-old Cuban boy from his relatives in Florida and whisk him away to an impoverished nation run by one of the last Communist dictators? Has President Bush used the Patriot Act to burn down a compound in Waco, Texas, killing many people—including children? I don't think so.

VRWC TALKING POINTS

★ We are at war with Islamic terrorists and we must treat them as battlefield combatants, not as common criminals entitled to constitutional rights.

★ The only "root cause" of Islamic terrorism is the spread of the credo of militant Islam.

★ Anyone who believes the September 11 attacks were an inside job belongs in an insane asylum next to some guy banging his head on the wall.

★ Militant Islamists don't want to change our policies; they want to turn us into an Islamic state.

★ Jihadists get their inspiration from the Koran. Acknowledging this fact makes you observant, not racist.

★ President Bush is fighting the terrorists for one reason—in order to defend America.

★ The Patriot Act allows the government to undertake vital, commonsense actions to help fight terrorism.

FEDERAL SPENDING: IN YOUR FACE AND OUT OF CONTROL

As we will see in Chapter 8, entitlements occupy a huge, unsustainable portion of the federal budget. But if you think that's the only example of extravagant government spending, then I have a "bridge to nowhere" to sell you. And it's an expensive one.

* * * * *

LIBERAL LUNACY:
"Our military campaigns justify bigger federal budgets."

"The era of a shrinking federal government has come to a close."[1] So declared New York senator Chuck Schumer in a *Washington Post* editorial exactly three months after the tragedy of September 11. His statement revealed the liberal agenda in the wake of the September 11 attacks: to expand the government under the guise of national security.

With the help of too many complacent Republicans—including President Bush—the liberals have achieved their goal. President Bush's proposed 2006 budget called for

$2.5 trillion in government spending, up 3.9 percent from the previous year. Congress, in its typical fashion, then approved $100 billion more than the president requested. Bush refused to veto these extra allocations. This should come as no surprise, seeing as Bush refused to veto a single bill for the first five years of his administration.

In fact, President Bush's budgets over the last five years have included average spending increases of 4.6 percent. But when all the extra funding by Congress gets piled on, the actual average increase comes to 7.8 percent.[2]

Liberals justify the ballooning budgets by arguing that they're necessary to fight the War on Terror. Like most liberal arguments, you should be careful about stepping into this one. Over the last five budgets, non-defense discretionary spending has grown at the exact same pace as the rest of the budget.[3] Thus, liberals are using the war in Iraq and other counter-terrorism measures to justify huge funding hikes in all areas. There's just nothing more exciting to a liberal than spending other people's money.

Liberal politicians will resort to some pretty tricky tactics to pass irresponsible spending measures. They'll even try to sneak them into bills meant for vital military spending, such as the U.S. Readiness, Veterans' Health and Iraq Accountability Act of 2007. Meant as an emergency supplemental bill to fund the troops in Iraq, congressional Democrats loaded this "war funding" bill with $3.7 billion in farm subsidies. These included $25 million for spinach growers, $252 million for milk subsidies, and a whopping $3.3 billion for crop and livestock losses due to natural disasters.[4] Democrats even added $74 million for peanut farmers. After widespread ridicule from Republicans and government watchdogs, some of the more obnoxious earmarks were stripped out of the bill, the final version of which, surprisingly, was vetoed by President Bush.

Winning the war one peanut at a time—there's the Democrats' motto for the War on Terror. Perhaps they can convince Jimmy Carter to lead the charge.

> **CONVERSATION STOPPER**
>
> Liberals are using the war in Iraq and other counterterrorism measures to justify huge funding hikes in all areas.

LIBERAL LUNACY:
"The U.S. needs to spend more to end African poverty."

If there's anything more annoying than liberal hectoring over our responsibility to end African poverty and disease, it's when that hectoring comes from millionaire celebrities. Led by U2 singer Bono, who apparently donated his last name to an African charity, the Hollywood crowd and much of the international Left have adopted the cause of ending African poverty as their latest fashionable crusade. Of course, none of this campaigning entails putting pressure on corrupt African dictators who ravage their own countries, destroy their own economies, and embezzle whatever international aid comes within a mile of their giant pockets. No, instead Africa's miseries are all America's fault, and it's we who must make amends and save the entire continent.

Take the Live 8 concert—a giant international music festival held across nine countries designed to pressure the G8 (read: America) to write off Africa's debt and fork over billions more in aid to the continent. At the concert, it went completely without mention that $40 billion of

African debt had already been written off before the concert even began. Likewise, President Bush's $15 billion program to fight AIDS in Africa—a tripling of U.S. aid to combat the scourge—was given short-shrift. In May 2007, President Bush proposed doubling the commitment to a $30 billion campaign to fight AIDS, mostly in Africa. The U.S. contribution is the biggest international health initiative dedicated to a specific disease.[5]

As former treasury secretary John Snow declared in 2005, "President Bush has tripled America's development assistance budget for Africa so that today nearly a quarter of every dollar of assistance in the region comes from America, when four years ago only 10 percent of assistance to the region came from America."[6] Naturally, all the government assistance is supplemented by the efforts of scores of private charities, a category in which the U.S. ranks as the most generous in the world.[7]

But does this largesse earn President Bush—or America for that matter—any credit from the international hand-wringers and professional sympathy mongers? Never. Liberals are convinced that if Africa is still dysfunctional, it's because America is simply not handing over enough money. The notion somehow eludes them that no amount of money will help a country when its dictator and his corrupt cronies steal all the funds.

And how bad is the problem of African corruption? Former Nigerian president Sani Abacha reportedly looted his own country of over $2 billion; the former president of Zaire, Mobutu Sese Seko, allegedly embezzled $5 billion. Corruption in Kenya is so bad that the former British high commissioner to Kenya, Edward Clay, accused Kenyan officials of being gluttonous on foreign aid to the point that they were "vomiting on the shoes" of donors.[8]

And that's not the worst of it. Nigeria's anti-corruption commission found that that country alone lost an astounding 220 billion pounds (approximately $450 billion) due to corruption between 1960 and 1999. That is nearly the equivalent of total Western aid given to Africa during that entire period. As the *Daily Telegraph* noted in 2005, "Gordon Brown, the [British] Chancellor, has spoken of a new Marshall Plan for Africa. But Nigeria's rulers have already pocketed the equivalent of six Marshall Plans."[9]

> **Even Bono Admits It**
>
> " This is the number one problem facing Africa—corruption; not natural calamity, not the AIDS virus. This is the number one issue and there's no way around it. "
>
> —Bono[10]

LIBERAL LUNACY:
"More education spending creates better education."

When companies fail to provide a desirable service to customers, they go out of business. But when a government program fails, the government gives it more money. That's what's happening with public schools today: the country's worst school districts like Washington, D.C., generally have the highest per-student spending. [11]

It's hard to argue that our education system is not well-funded. Between 1965 and 2002, federal education spending skyrocketed from $25 billion (adjusted for inflation) to over $108 billion, entailing a near-tripling of per-pupil funding when state and local spending is included. And what have we gotten in return for this massive investment? According to a CATO analysis, "Math and reading scores have stagnated, graduation rates have flatlined, and researchers have shown numerous billion-dollar federal programs to be failures."[12]

And the government's solution to this situation? Why, throw more money at the problem, of course. With the enthusiastic support of Ted Kennedy, President Bush in 2002 signed the No Child Left Behind Act, attempting to improve education by imposing new—and expensive—standards on government-funded schools, and effectively creating an entire new bureaucracy to monitor compliance. Bush requested $24.4 billion for the program for 2008, a 41 percent increase over the program's original cost in 2001.[13]

The situation in higher education is no better. Federal financial aid for college students jumped from $19 billion in 1990 to $63 billion in 2000, while the proportion of the U.S. population going to college was barely affected. Meanwhile, studies show that the average college senior studies just thirteen hours per week, and nearly half of full-time college students fail to graduate within six years.[14] I'm reminded of Bluto's exclamation in *Animal House*: "Seven years of college down the drain!" Except that in the movie, the line was meant as a joke.

It doesn't take a Ph.D. to see that ever-increasing federal funding of education yields a poor return on investment. What's more, politicians use the massive education spending bills to hide earmarks for their favorite supporters. A good example is the spending bill that emerged from a Senate committee on June 21, 2007, which included a $1 million allocation requested by senators Hillary Clinton and Charles Schumer for a museum commemorating the 1969 Woodstock concert.[15] That's right—a million bucks of your tax money to glorify 500,000 stoned hippies rolling around in mud. That's $2 per hippy, for those of you keeping count.

Your Education Dollars at Work

The federal government has given:[16]

- $8.5 million for whaling museums, "heritage centers," and other projects meant to support "culturally based educational activities, internships, apprenticeship programs, and exchanges for Alaska Natives, Native Hawaiians, and children and families of Massachusetts."

- nearly half a million dollars combined to two projects. The first is a California project that shows how to use *basketry* to improve academic instruction in areas like math. The second project, in Oakland, pays for senior citizens to engage in "storytelling, oral history, and intergenerational theater" for poor elementary school students.

- nearly $1 billion in 2004 alone (up from $847,000 just nine years earlier) to after school programs called "21st Century Community Learning Centers." In January 2003, the Department of Education reported that the centers "had limited influence on academic performance, no influence on feelings of safety or on the number of 'latchkey' children and some negative influences on behavior."

LIBERAL LUNACY:
"We need government spending to close the gaps between the haves and the have-nots."

According to John Edwards, there are two Americas—a rich one and one that's struggling just to get by. And how do we lift up the struggling America? Through government programs, of course!

Economic freedom, not a government redistribution of wealth, gives people the best chance to succeed—period. Free markets, by harnessing the individual initiative and intelligence of millions of people, cause an upward march in the quality of life and standard of living for *everyone*. Technological innovations in particular promote material equality better than anything else.

Capitalism and international free trade have created a rising wave of global prosperity—one of the biggest stories you've never read. Instead, the media likes to trumpet predictions of imminent global catastrophe; Al Gore's *Earth in the Balance* seems to be required reading in journalism schools. But are we really heading toward doomsday? A 2007 UN report, "State of the Future," found that thanks to capitalism, "People around the world are becoming healthier, wealthier, better educated, more peaceful, more connected, and they are living longer." The percentage of the world population living on less than $1 a day fell from 40 percent in 1981 to 25 percent today, adjusted for inflation. The report further predicted that if current growth rates continue, "world poverty will be cut in half between 2000 and 2015." Stephen Moore rightly calls this "arguably one of the greatest triumphs in human history."[17]

The free market of ideas and technology, not the government, is closing the gap between the rich and the poor.

According to one study: "Today the typical American, defined as poor by the government, has a refrigerator, a stove, a clothes washer, a car, air conditioning, a VCR, a microwave, a stereo, and a color TV. He is able to obtain medical care and his home is in good repair and is not over-crowded. By his own report, his family is not hungry and in the last year he had sufficient funds to meet his essential needs. While this individual's life is not opulent, it is equally far from the popular images of poverty conveyed by politicians, the press, and activists."[18] In fact, "the principal nutrition-related problem facing the poor in America is obesity, not hunger; the poor have a higher rate of obesity than other socioeconomic groups. . . . Nearly 40 percent of the households defined as poor by the U.S. government actually own their own homes" and "poor" Americans have "more housing space and are less likely to be overcrowded than the average citizen in Western Europe."[19]

LIBERAL LUNACY:
"Unlike the private sector, the government is motivated by public interest."

Hardly! Businesses give far more to society than do most government projects, and the private sector is far more accountable to the public than the federal government is. If people are dissatisfied with a private company, they stop patronizing it and the company loses money. Government, conversely, gets its income by leveling taxes. And you can't stop paying taxes when you're dissatisfied with the government's performance.

Businesses provide us with jobs, places to eat, live, and shop, and even life-saving drugs. Businesses do not get their customers the same way the government does. People go to the government because there's nowhere else to get a driver's license or apply for a building permit. People frequent business establishments *voluntarily* and only those businesses that have something they *want*. Bill Gates is rich today because his innovative ideas and products have put computing powers into more hands for less money.

Liberals howl at the "selfish" motivations of economically successful citizens because they fail to see the tremendous benefits society receives from the efforts of these "selfish" people. Our lives today are better than they were ten years ago thanks to these entrepreneurs who through hard work and creative thinking provided us with technology such as computers, cell phones, and DVDs.

And let's talk about the self-anointed "selfless, public-interest oriented" liberals to whom we're supposed to be grateful for bestowing their wonderful social spending on us. Remember when John Edwards charged the taxpayer-funded University of California at Davis $55,000 for a single speech—about *poverty*? Remember the press reports revealing that Al Gore's Tennessee mansion uses twenty times more electricity than the average household? What about those "selfless" public school teachers unions who jealously protect their inflated salaries, fight all proposals for merit-based pay, and relentlessly try to thwart school choice initiatives that would force them to compete with other schools? And of course, I suppose that the American Federation of Government Employees, as the largest federal employee labor union, just exists to advance the public interest—not the interests of its members.

If everyone in America woke up tomorrow and decided they wanted to work for the government, they could not. Why? Because there would be no one to pay the salaries. Without a private sector to create wealth, goods, and services, the government cannot do anything and cannot spend anything. A thriving private sector is thus essential to the well-being of the public sector.

VRWC TALKING POINTS

★ Liberals will use any excuse, even military necessity, to get approval for more government spending.

★ America's massive foreign aid program for Africa will continue to be ineffective as long as corrupt African dictators keep mismanaging their economies and stealing our aid.

★ Constant increases in government spending on education have not improved the education system. Some problems can't be solved by just throwing more money at them.

★ The free market is a much more reliable means of fighting poverty than government spending.

★ The government is not a selfless charity. Government bureaucracies zealously pursue their own interests.

THE COURTS:
AN OLIGARCHY IN ROBES

Liberals know that their social agenda, consisting largely of abortion-on-demand and same-sex marriage, is wildly unpopular with the American people. Unable to implement their policies through democratic means (you know, elections), they turned to the courts, where they found a convenient way to pass radical new laws without the approval of "we the people." What can we do about it? Elect a president who will appoint conservative judges who respect the Constitution!

* * * * *

LIBERAL LUNACY:
"We need activist courts to institute
same-sex marriage."

Liberal judges understand the Supreme Court's authority to "interpret the law" as a license to *make* the law. In their own defense, these judges explain that they're keeping the Constitution "current" with the "changing times." Or in Al Gore's words, the Constitution is a "living, breathing document." (How exactly does a document "live" and "breathe," anyway? Do you have to feed it?) Actually, the

Framers of the Constitution contemplated the need for change by permitting amendments under Article V. True, it is not easy to obtain the consensus of society needed to amend the Constitution. So liberals have taken to the guise of this "living Constitution" to advance their agenda without having to suffer the inconvenience of submitting their actions to a vote.

By far, the liberals' most audacious effort to thwart the will of the American people is their campaign to get the courts to impose same-sex marriage. In 2003, four judges on the Massachusetts Supreme Court tossed aside the state's three-hundred-year-old definition of marriage as a legal union between a man and a woman, calling the law "irrational." That's right, in a single decision, four judges eliminated a law dating back to the eighteenth century without any concern for the opinion of the other 6.5 million Massachusetts residents about the divisive political issue of same-sex marriage. In early 2004, the court clarified that allowing civil unions was not enough—the state must extend full marriage rights to homosexuals.

While Massachusetts remains the only state with legalized same-sex marriage, courts in other states such as California, Vermont, New Jersey, and Iowa have ordered the establishment of same-sex civil unions or outright same-sex marriage. Some of these rulings are being appealed, although Vermont and New Jersey have complied with the courts' commands and mandated civil unions. Only two states—Connecticut and New Hampshire— have approved civil unions without being forced to do so by the courts. Legislators in Washington and a few other states, however, have approved "domestic partnerships" or other, lesser kinds of same-sex marriage benefits.

Based largely on the judicial activism displayed in Massachusetts, citizens organized nationwide to hold referenda to ban same-sex marriage—in other words, to prevent activist courts from imposing the institution on an unwilling population. These referenda have proved extremely successful, winning approval in all eleven states that held them during the 2004 presidential election. These measures passed by a 2-to-1 ratio overall, with large majorities expressing support for traditional marriage even in liberal states like Oregon.[1] In the 2006 elections, similar initiatives passed in seven of the eight states that held them. Twenty-seven states now have adopted constitutional amendments to ban same-sex marriage, while forty-two states have some kind of law prohibiting it.[2] When the people—and not a handful of judges—are given a chance to vote on this issue, they almost always vote against same-sex marriage. This shows that same-sex marriage is really only supported by a fringe group of radical judges and left-wing activists. Even Bill Clinton signed the Defense of Marriage Act, which prohibits the federal government from recognizing same sex marriages and allows states to choose not to recognize same-sex marriages performed in other states.

The issue is not really about same-sex marriage per se. It's about the Left's attempt to subvert the intent of America's founders, who gave ultimate power to "we the people," not some men in black robes. If the question of the "right" to same-sex marriage were left to the American people, it would become a non-issue (just like the "right" to other oxymorons like "jumbo shrimp," "recorded live," or "French deodorant.") The American people time and again have declared that marriage should remain as the union of one man and one woman, and not the union of one man and six women, one woman and a hamster, two women, or a woman and an alien (sorry, Michael Jackson). And why is same-sex marriage even necessary at all? Nothing prevents gays, lesbians, ambisexuals, or even metrosexuals from entering into all sorts of contractual rights, drawing up living wills, buying life insurance, purchasing property jointly, or memorializing their relationships in many other ways. But whether their arrangements should be sanctioned with the name of marriage must be decided by "we the people," not "they the judges."

LIBERAL LUNACY:
"The Supreme Court can be relied upon to uphold the Constitution."

Judges have a disturbing tendency to "grow" into liberals once they get make it to the Supreme Court. Enjoying lifetime appointments with no accountability, liberal justices have turned the Court into a kind of supreme legislature. They enact laws that not only have nothing to do with interpreting the Constitution, but oftentimes directly contradict the Constitution itself.

This trend is nothing new. The most notorious example of the Supreme Court's judicial activism is the 1973 *Roe v. Wade* decision, in which the Court struck down laws prohibiting abortion on the grounds of an imagined Constitutional "right to privacy." Where exactly is the "right to the privacy" in the Constitution—or the "right to abortion," for that matter? Read the document! You won't find them. You'll find the words "arms" and "property," but not "privacy" or "abortion."

But the liberal activists on the Supreme Court won't be stopped, even when their decisions contradict the

Constitution's *explicit words*. In 2003, the Supreme Court upheld some of the blatantly unconstitutional provisions of the McCain-Feingold campaign finance reform bill, including the ban on unions, corporations, and interest groups from broadcasting certain kinds of political ads shortly before a primary or general election. According to the First Amendment, "Congress shall make no law . . . abridging the freedom of speech, or of the press." McCain-Feingold, of course, abridges *both* these freedoms, but hey, it's Constitutional—because the Supreme Court says so. Or at least, it said so until the Court effectively overruled itself in 2007 and struck down much of this law after Justices Roberts and Alito were added to the bench.

Not satisfied with merely assaulting our political rights, the Supreme Court also gave two big thumbs up to racial discrimination in the form of "affirmative action." In *Grutter v. Bollinger* (2003), the Court upheld the use of affirmative action—in other words, reverse discrimination—by universities in their admissions processes. Although the Fourteenth Amendment guarantees "equal protection of the laws," the justices apparently approve of the government's habit of finding some races to be more equal than others.

A final outrage by our top court came in the form of the *Kelo v. City of New London* decision in 2005, which expanded the bounds of eminent domain to allow local governments to confiscate private property and turn it over to private developers. The Fifth Amendment limits eminent domain to land intended for "public use," but the Supreme Court seems to have concluded that when the Constitution's Framers said "public," they really meant "public or private." Thank goodness for liberal justices— what would we do without heroes like Stephen Breyer and

Ruth Bader Ginsburg to tell us that the Framers didn't really mean what they wrote?

There's only one solution to liberal judicial activism—elect a president in 2008 that will appoint conservative judges to the courts.

LIBERAL LUNACY:
"The Supreme Court should consult international law in its rulings."

In recent years, the Supreme Court has become increasingly enamored of international law. In *Thompson v. Oklahoma* (1988), Justice Stevens invoked the examples of a variety of foreign nations in ruling against the application of the death penalty to a juvenile murderer. He even cited the Soviet Union, as if the U.S. has something to learn about human rights from a totalitarian empire. More recently, in *Lawrence v. Texas* (2003), Justice Kennedy cited the European Court of Human Rights in support of the Supreme Court's decision to abolish a Texas law outlawing homosexual sodomy. Before her retirement, Justice O'Connor specifically endorsed the citation of international law, declaring that "although international law and the law of other nations are rarely binding upon our decisions in U.S. courts, conclusions reached by other countries and by the international community should at times constitute persuasive authority in American courts."[3] Justice Ginsburg has even extolled foreign law as a means to fight discrimination: "We are losers if we neglect what others can tell us about endeavors to eradicate bias against women, minorities and other disadvantaged groups," she proclaimed.[4]

Why are the highest justices of our court system looking to foreign countries and international courts for guid-
ance in establishing American law? Their job is to interpret
the U.S. Constitution, not to troll foreign courts for trendy
international legal norms. It's bad enough that liberal
justices subscribe to the view of a "living Constitution."
But in citing international law, some judges have abandoned even the pretense of fulfilling their oath to per-
form their duties "under the Constitution and laws of the
United States."

Justice Scalia has noted how Supreme Court judges se-
lectively cite foreign law whenever it helps their cause.
For example, in *Lawrence v. Texas*, liberal justices invoked
countries where homosexual sodomy is not criminalized.
However, Scalia observed, the United States has some of
the most liberal abortion laws in the world, and yet none
of the Supreme Court justices ever argue that U.S. abortion law should be more restrictive because that's the international norm.[5] In other words, liberal justices cite
international law whenever it helps forward their agenda.
Go figure.

The consideration of international law by U.S. judges is
an extremely dangerous development. The United States
is a unique country with its own traditions and legal code.
We do not share all the values of the "international community," where barbaric customs such as female genital
mutilation and, in some countries, even slavery are still prac-
ticed. The incorporation of international law into the U.S.
legal system represents a dangerous infringement of our
sovereignty. It is an effort to move the country away from
the clear mandates of the Constitution toward the more
liberal mores of foreign courts and international opinion.

Justices Scalia and Thomas on the Supreme Court's Invocation of International Law

- Justice Scalia: "Equally irrelevant are the practices of the 'world community,' whose notions of justice are (thankfully) not always those of our people. We must never forget that it is a Constitution for the United States of America that we are expounding. . . . [W]here there is not first a settled consensus among our own people, the views of other nations, however enlightened the Justices of this Court may think them to be, cannot be imposed upon Americans through the Constitution.' "[6]

- Justice Thomas: "While Congress, as a *legislature*, may wish to consider the actions of other nations on any issue it likes, this Court's Eighth Amendment jurisprudence should not impose foreign moods, fads, or fashions on Americans."[7]

- Justice Scalia: "If you talk about using [international law in] constitutional law, you talk about how it's nice to know that we're on the right track, that we have the same moral and legal framework as the rest of the world. But we don't have the same moral and legal framework as the rest of the world, and we never have. If you told the Framers of the Constitution that what we're after is to do something that will be just like Europe, they would have been appalled. And if you read the *Federalist Papers*, it's full of statements that make very clear that they didn't have a whole lot of respect for many of the rules in European countries."[8]

LIBERAL LUNACY:
"The courts must enforce the separation of Church and state."

ACLU lawyers make their living by insisting that the smallest sign of religion in public life today represents an unconstitutional breach of the "separation of Church and state." Courts increasingly agree with these anti-Christian zealots, banning everything from Christmas trees in school lobbies to displays of the Ten Commandments in courthouses. The issue has also intruded on the debate over school vouchers, where opponents of school choice consistently try to ban parochial schools from participating in voucher programs.

Doesn't anyone actually read the Constitution anymore? The First Amendment's Establishment Clause, which is what these lawsuits and judgments usually cite, instructs that "Congress shall make no law respecting an establishment of religion, or prohibiting the free exercise thereof." The Framers' intent was to prevent the U.S. government from creating a national religion or state church like the Anglican Church in England, not to drag grandma into court for erecting a nativity scene in the neighborhood park.

The furious effort to banish religion from public life hit a low point in 2002, when a three-judge panel of the notoriously liberal Ninth Circuit Court of Appeals, located in Nancy Pelosi's San Francisco, ruled that the recitation of the Pledge of Allegiance was unconstitutional in public schools because it included the phrase "under God." Once in a while, judges grow so out-of-touch with the people and so arrogant in their power that they provoke a backlash. This was one of those times. The ruling outraged Americans coast to coast. The U.S. Senate unanimously passed a resolution condemning the ruling, which was eventually overturned by the Supreme Court on a procedural point.

The entire notion of a "wall of separation" between Church and state is nowhere to be found in the Constitution. This claim is based on a letter written by Thomas Jefferson to a Baptist community in Connecticut a decade after the First Amendment was ratified. As Kevin Gutzman has noted, "Thomas Jefferson played no role in drafting or adopting the Establishment Clause. He was neither a member of the first Congress that drafted the First Amendment . . . nor a member of the Virginia General Assembly that voted to ratify it."[9] Why have the courts attributed such crucial importance to a personal letter that was little noticed for decades after it was written? Because, much to the dismay of the ACLU, nothing in the Constitution calls for the banishment of religion from public life. To the contrary, the Constitution's Framers generally believed in God and viewed religion as a vital inspiration for good government.

As Thomas Jefferson himself asked rhetorically, "Can the liberties of a nation be thought secure when we have removed their only firm basis, a conviction in the minds of the people that these liberties are the gift of God? That they are not violated but with his wrath?"[10]

So we're left with two views on this issue:

Thomas Jefferson: All our liberties are a gift from God.

The ACLU: Invoking God in public life is unconstitutional and dangerous.

Whose side are you on?

LIBERAL LUNACY:
"Tort law helps the little guy against companies that place profit over people and consumer safety."

This argument fails to recognize the fundamental truth that, in terms of our vulnerability in our litigation-happy society, most of us are "companies." Whether we work at the companies as employees, run the companies as managers, buy from companies as customers, or hold stocks in companies for our retirement, virtually every one of us is dependent upon business in one way or another. Nearly all the food, clothes, housing and entertainment we buy every day come from businesses and people trying to earn a profit. Simply put, American companies are you, me, and even our liberal friends—who hit up private companies for donations and siphon off their taxes to pay for zany social programs.

Of course, a company seeks to make a profit. That's its whole point for existing. If, however, it tries to make a profit by making slipshod or dangerous products, you don't need to get a lawyer to make things right. The marketplace will make the company pay in lost sales and bad publicity. A company has no incentive to kill or hurt its customers. Remember: no government regulation was needed to remove the Edsel from Ford's production line. Likewise, companies now use safety as a selling point: check out the ad campaigns for every liberal's favorite set of wheels, the Volvo, or every liberal's favorite whipping boy, the SUV.

Or look what happened with tainted Chinese products. In 2007, U.S. stores recalled a host of defective and dangerous Chinese-made products, including foods, fireworks, pet foods, and toys. Suddenly, a lot of people didn't want to buy anything that was made in China. So what happened? Did we need lawyers to sue the bejeezus out of companies and bankrupt them in order to teach them a lesson? No, because companies, responding to consumer demands, acted on their own accord. As people demanded "not made in China" products, companies made money by supplying them. Non-China products were usually more expensive, but companies switched suppliers anyway, because people were willing to pay more for safer products.[11] Companies that sold unsafe Chinese-made products suffered, and those that sold safer, non-Chinese products made money. There was no need for bureaucrats, lawyers, or government regulators, because the free market is largely self-regulating. And we should note, of course, that the original tainted products made it onto the shelves despite reams of government safety regulations that clearly do not work.

Tort lawsuits have become the newest form of the lottery. Litigants know they can win millions with the right case—and potential defendants know it too. In personal negligence cases, the average award continues to rise, now exceeding $3 million.[12]

If you want an example of how out of control our tort system is, just look at the unhinged Roy Pearson, who sued a dry cleaners for $67 million—for losing his pants. At the trial in June 2007, Pearson broke down on the stand and needed a break to compose himself after describing the anguish he supposedly suffered due to his lost pants. This spectacle was ridiculous, but it was no laughing matter for the defendants, two Korean immigrants who had to shell out tens of thousands of dollars in legal costs to fight the deranged pants man. In the end, they only managed to pay off their legal bills thanks to donations from sympathizers. And the worst part of the case? Roy Pearson was a Washington, D.C., judge.[13]

The overall cost to our economy of the litigation fetish is huge. In March 2007, the free-market think tank Pacific

Research Institute published a study revealing that America's tort system imposes a staggering annual cost of $865 billion on the U.S. economy. That is equivalent to an annual "tort tax" of $9,827 for a family of four. Lawsuits cause companies to shed $684 billion annually in shareholder value, while cutbacks in research and development stemming from litigation expenses cost them over $367 billion in lost sales every year.[14]

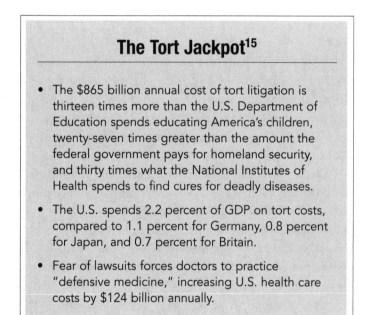

The Tort Jackpot[15]

- The $865 billion annual cost of tort litigation is thirteen times more than the U.S. Department of Education spends educating America's children, twenty-seven times greater than the amount the federal government pays for homeland security, and thirty times what the National Institutes of Health spends to find cures for deadly diseases.

- The U.S. spends 2.2 percent of GDP on tort costs, compared to 1.1 percent for Germany, 0.8 percent for Japan, and 0.7 percent for Britain.

- Fear of lawsuits forces doctors to practice "defensive medicine," increasing U.S. health care costs by $124 billion annually.

LIBERAL LUNACY:
"We need tort law to punish negligent doctors and greedy drug companies."

Conservatives don't want to abolish the tort system. Certainly people and companies who hurt people, intentionally or unintentionally, should pay a price. But a system designed to hold individuals and companies accountable for their wrongdoing is different from a system in which defendants can be financially destroyed by the mere cost of being sued or by a runaway jury.

In our litigious culture, juries have immense power but no accountability. Should it be this way? Should a randomly selected set of eight unelected, unaccountable jurors in a single town have the lawful power to ruin a doctor's practice or drive a pharmaceutical company into bankruptcy?

Let's say a company spends tens of millions of dollars researching, inventing, and testing a new drug to cure a life-threatening disease. After shepherding the drug through an approval process that takes many years with the U.S. Food and Drug Administration, the drug is approved and sold to the public. Ten years pass as the drug amasses a reputation as a real lifesaver. But then, two plaintiffs sue the company, claiming that its scientists failed to identify a dangerous side effect of the drug. At the trial, a jury (none of whom are scientists or attended college) decides that the company's scientists made serious mistakes. It awards the plaintiff $3 million in compensatory damages and $50 million in punitive damages. This verdict bankrupts the company. The life-saving drug is taken off the market.

Is America better off? Thanks to runaway lawsuits, helpful drugs get pulled off the shelves or have their prices ratcheted up sky-high in order to cover liability costs. Liability costs now account for over 90 percent of the price of childhood vaccines, resulting in a drop in the number of children being vaccinated by an estimated 1 million.[16]

The outrageous financial penalties extracted from doctors accused of malpractice has taken a severe toll on our health care system. According to the American Medical Association, the median medical liability jury award in medical liability cases nearly tripled from 1997 to 2004, rising from $157,000 to $439,400. This has driven malpractice insurance rates sky-high. As a result, 45 percent of hospitals reported that the professional liability crisis has led to the loss of doctors and/or reduced emergency coverage. The AMA says that twenty-one states are now experiencing a medical liability crisis. Just in Florida, neurosurgeons have cut back on emergency care, seven hospitals have closed down their obstetrics units, and more than half of the rural doctors reported that they had cut back on risky procedures like childbirth, all due to the fear of lawsuits or inability to afford malpractice insurance.[17]

So who do we want to run out of town? The doctors who treat us when we're sick, or the lawyers who make millions suing them?

VRWC TALKING POINTS

★ Liberals turn to the courts to implement same-sex marriage because the vast majority of Americans oppose it when they're allowed a say.

★ Liberal Supreme Court judges have long served as handmaidens to America's Left by legislating their political agenda from the bench. The only solution is to elect a president who will appoint conservative justices.

★ The citation of international law by liberal Supreme Court justices is a threat to American sovereignty.

★ The Constitution does *not* call for a "wall of separation" between Church and state.

★ Tort law allows for frivolous lawsuits and outrageously high jury awards that cost the economy billions of dollars every year.

★ Because of the tort system, life-saving doctors and drug companies are being driven out of business.

TAXES: THE ONLY LEGAL FORM OF THEFT

Liberals have never met a tax they didn't like. That's because every one of their pet social programs costs money. Someone has to pay for bad little ideas like Hillary Clinton's proposed "service academy" for training future bureaucrats. And someone has to pay even more for bad big ideas like John Edwards' universal health care plan. So where's the cash going to come from? You guessed it—from YOUR pockets.

* * * * *

LIBERAL LUNACY:
"Bush's tax cuts were tax cuts for the rich."

There's something about tax policy that really brings out liberals' tendency toward class warfare. In left-wing circles, Bush's tax cuts have been roundly condemned as "tax cuts for the rich." Ah yes, those evil rich people again. If we could only get rid of all the rich people, then we'd be left with—lots of poor people. As Winston Churchill once said, "The inherent vice of capitalism is the unequal sharing of blessings; the inherent virtue of socialism is the equal sharing of miseries."

Bush's tax cuts, among other measures, lowered the marginal income, capital gains, and dividend tax rates, and they reduced the marriage penalty and estate taxes. Liberals should actually support this package, because in the end the rich ended up paying an even higher share of the total tax burden than before. According to a 2007 study by the Heritage Foundation, "Since 2000, the share of individual income taxes paid by the bottom 40 percent of taxpayers dropped from zero to minus 4 percent—meaning the average family in this group got a subsidy from the refundable child tax credit or earned income tax credit. The share of income taxes paid by the top fifth of taxpayers climbed from 81 percent to 85 percent."[1]

So the poorest Americans went from paying nothing to actually getting a subsidy, but liberals still oppose Bush's tax cuts because the "rich" got some relief, too. For liberals, wealth is a zero-sum game—the only way the poor can get some money is to take it away from the rich. It's no surprise that every major Democratic presidential candidate has proposed to reverse some or all of Bush's tax cuts or allow them to expire.

Bush's tax cuts, much like Ronald Reagan's, were a great economic stimulus. (It's funny how people tend to work harder and become more ambitious whenever you let them keep more of their own income.) Since the Bush tax cuts were introduced, the economy has expanded robustly. The unemployment rate in January 2007 was the second lowest since the mid-1970s[2]—so much for liberal whining about a "jobless recovery."

What's more, the tax cuts paid for themselves. Capital gains tax revenues doubled after the capital gains tax was reduced,[3] while overall tax receipts have risen 37 percent over the previous three years.[4] As conservatives have always argued, tax cuts actually increase tax revenues by increasing economic growth.

Nevertheless, Democrats have campaigned heavily on the tax issue, vowing to refuse to renew the tax cuts when they begin to expire in 2010. In light of the Bush tax cuts' undeniable success, it's clear that liberals' problem

---

Which Party Can You Trust on April 15?

" President Bush yesterday signed into law his third tax cut in as many years. "

Washington Post, 2003[5]

" In ending what [Hillary Clinton] called Mr. Bush's 'irresponsible' tax cuts, the former first lady said she would revert to the tax rates for 'upper-income Americans' during the 1990s. "

—*New York Sun*, 2007[6]

" Democratic presidential candidate John Edwards yesterday issued a blueprint aimed at providing health-care coverage for all Americans and said he would raise taxes to help pay the roughly $100 billion annual bill. "

—*Washington Post*, 2007[7]

" Democratic presidential hopeful Barack Obama on Tuesday offered a plan to provide health care to millions of Americans and more affordable medical insurance, financed by tax increases on the wealthy. "

—*Chicago Sun-Times*, 2007[8]

with tax relief is not so much economic as it is ideological. They want more government control over the economy because they're afraid Americans will spend their own money on the "wrong" things, such as SUVs, guns, or red meat. Instead, liberals want the government to confiscate our hard-earned money and spend it on their own pet causes, like vegan lunches and unisex bathrooms for United Nations delegates.

LIBERAL LUNACY:
"We need higher taxes on the profits of greedy oil companies."

In February 2007, Exxon announced a $39.5 billion annual profit.[9] What was the liberals' reaction? Were they happy that a U.S. company had been so successful while employing thousands of workers, paying billions in taxes, and supplying the market with a vital product? Not quite. Hillary Clinton summed up the liberal response when she declared, "The other day the oil companies reported the highest profits in the history of the world. I want to take those profits and I want to put them into a strategic energy fund. . . ."[10]

Oil companies are making money? How dare they!

This is the typical liberal reaction when they see anyone they don't like make a buck; "Confiscate it!" they say. And they're especially insistent when the target is a politically incorrect company like an oil firm. When was the last time you heard liberals demand that the government confiscate Birkenstock's profits?

So the price of gas rises to $3 a gallon, and the Hillary choir demands that the government steal oil companies' profits and put them into a "strategic energy fund" which, conveniently, politicians like Hillary would control. Once again, companies must be punished for being successful and their profits turned over to the government, which supposedly knows better how to spend that money than does the company that earned it in the first place.

It's true that we should reduce our dependence on foreign oil. But is Hillary Clinton really the best person to oversee a massive centrally planned program to confiscate oil companies' wealth? Is Hillary—or any other politician for that matter—the most qualified economist to decide what are the best sources of alternative energy, which should receive state subsidies, and how much should be given to each?

But if this kind of central planning doesn't work—and seventy years of economic misery in the Soviet Union is a pretty strong indication that it doesn't—then what could encourage the development of alternative energy sources? I have an idea—it's pretty controversial in this day and age, but I say we give it a shot. It's called the free market.

And in a free market, high oil prices are a great incentive to encourage creative entrepreneurs to develop alternative energy. The higher the price of oil, the more potential profit there is for a businessman or company to develop and market a cheaper energy source. We don't even need a giant government program to subsidize ethanol or any other alternative energy source. If there's a buck to be made by developing alternative energy, companies will do it.

If liberals are really so concerned by the price of oil, then why don't they let us build new oil refineries? Thanks to strict environmental regulations, no one has built a new refinery in America since 1976. And thanks to Democratic senators and congressmen, repeated efforts to approve drilling for oil in Alaska's Arctic National Wildlife Refuge

(ANWR) have failed. Liberals would prefer to keep us dependent on oil from Saudi Islamic radicals and neo-communist crackpots like Venezuela's Hugo Chavez than risk disturbing the psychic serenity of a few caribou.

Unfortunately, it takes a long time to build new refineries and to extract oil from new sites. Sure, in the meantime, no one likes paying high gas prices. But no one likes paying for anything. Maybe some day liberals will succeed in creating a moneyless utopia where everything you want miraculously appears on pristine shore shelves and carries a colorful price tag that says "$0." But until then, punishing successful oil companies by confiscating their profits will achieve nothing except to *raise* the price of gas, since companies will have less incentive to increase the oil supply if they make less money doing it.

If the government really wants to give some immediate relief to gas consumers, instead of attacking oil companies, why doesn't it just reduce, or better yet, abolish the enormous taxes it levies on gasoline? Combined local, state, and federal gas taxes amount to an average of 45.9 cents per gallon.[11]

You want to pay less for gas? Then drive that SUV over to city hall and tell them to eliminate the gas tax.

> **Common Sense on Taxes**
>
> " You can't control the economy without controlling the people. "
>
> —Ronald Reagan
>
> " The soundest way to raise revenues in the long run is to cut taxes now. The purpose of cutting taxes now is . . . to achieve the more prosperous, expanding economy which can bring a budget surplus. "
>
> —John F. Kennedy

LIBERAL LUNACY:

"A progressive tax code is the fairest kind of tax code."

Fair? Our wonderful, "progressive" tax code, in fact, is a nine-million word behemoth that's about as comprehensible as *War and Peace* translated into Sanskrit.

Of course the tax code isn't fair. It's so complicated that Americans face annual tax compliance costs of around $265 billion.[12] Accountants have created an entire industry to figure out all the obscure loopholes and deductions so that taxpayers don't end up paying even more than they have to.

All liberals have to offer on tax policy is tinkering at the margins—mostly finding new ways to raise taxes on the "rich," however they define that category at any given time. It's probably useless to hope for more comprehensive tax reform from liberals—a progressive income tax, after all, was one of the ten key steps Karl Marx outlined in *The Communist Manifesto* in order to abolish capitalism.

But in recent years, we've seen two daring proposals from conservatives for a comprehensive overhaul of our antiquated tax system. The time has arrived to give these ideas serious consideration.

The first is the flat tax. As described by its most enthusiastic champion, Steve Forbes, the flat tax would abolish progressive personal and corporate income taxes, taxes on capital gains, dividends, interest, and estates, and most deductions. These would be replaced by a flat tax of 17 percent on both personal and corporate income, along with the retention of a select few deductions and exemptions for children, married couples, and the poor. That's it— nearly everyone pays a straight 17 percent. Not only would the flat tax lower taxes for people of all income levels, but it would replace our entire Byzantine tax system with a simple new one that would allow people to file all their federal taxes on a postcard. As Forbes notes, his ideas have encountered a lot of resistance from accountancies like H&R Block, which would stand to lose millions if taxes were made so simple that people could calculate and file them themselves.[13]

The second proposal is capably advocated by Neal Boortz and Congressman John Linder in their book, *The FairTax Book*.[14] The fair tax would essentially overthrow the entire federal tax scheme in favor of a 23 percent retail sales tax on new goods and services. Current taxes on corporate and individual income, the alternative minimum tax, the death tax, taxes on capital gains, Social Security and Medicare taxes, as well as all kinds of hidden taxes would be completely eliminated. Every family would receive a monthly "prebate" to cover the amount of the sales tax paid to the federal poverty level. The downside of the flat tax is that implementing it would likely require the repeal of the Sixteenth Amendment, which allows the government to collect an income tax. Otherwise, the most likely outcome is that eventually we'd end up with both a national sales *and* an income tax. The upside, however, is pretty enticing—the fair tax would effectively abolish the IRS.

The efforts to pass the flat tax and the fair tax show that conservatives are thinking big about tax reform. In contrast, all the liberals have to offer is more of the same old "soak the rich" shtick. Seeing that so many liberal politicians are millionaires themselves, it's hard to believe that they even believe their own rhetoric. After all, if the current tax system doesn't take enough from the rich, then why don't Ted Kennedy, John Edwards, and all the other liberal plutocrats just *offer* to pay more themselves?

LIBERAL LUNACY:
"High taxes enable the government to build infrastructure and create jobs."

Nope, sorry. Read my lips: the government does not create jobs. Liberals frequently defend government spending by pointing to its ostensible visible effects. Liberal politicians who want to take your money for some alleged "greater good" can point to a government-funded bridge or school and boast about the marvels of governmental works. But they don't tell you about the invisible costs of such government spending.[15] To build a bridge or a school, the government needs to get money from somewhere. After all, the government has no money of its own. To raise money for government works, the tax collector takes money from you and me and the rest of the productive private sector. We pay for government projects through our taxes.

And how do taxpayers manage to pay their tax bills? By working. In taking money from taxpayers for a project deemed worthy by some politician, the government is depriving the taxpayers of the fruits of their labor. If they had been allowed to keep their money, they would have spent it and strengthened the economy—which *really* creates jobs. Every dollar the government takes from me is one less dollar I have to spend on a home, a car, or on my family. We can see the bridge or school the government built with our money, but we don't see those people who remain unemployed because, due to my high tax bill, I couldn't buy a new home, a new car, or send my child to private school.

LIBERAL LUNACY:
"We need high taxes in order to provide for the poor."

Why is it right for some government bureaucrat to decide when and how and to what extent I care for the needy? Economist Leonard Read explains: "It is absurd for me forcibly to impose my will upon you: dictate what you are to discover, invent, create, where you shall work, the hours of your labor, the wage you shall receive, what and with whom you shall exchange. And it is just as absurd," he continues, for government "to try to forcibly direct and control your creative or productive or peaceful actions."[16] This is true even for a good cause like caring for the poor.

Nevertheless, largely in the name of caring for the poor, today the top 5 percent of income earners in the U.S. pay over half (57 percent) of the federal income tax, while the bottom half pays hardly anything (3.3 percent).[17] Thus the great burden of income tax is imposed on a relatively small percentage of the nation's income earners. Taking a substantial portion of income from those in society who are the most productive is not only unfair, it's harmful to those who are supposed to benefit from the government's benevolence.

Who will provide jobs for the unemployed or the poor, other than those who have the financial and intellectual wherewithal to start businesses, create jobs, and yes, even pay taxes? Remember, there are no employees without employers. As Ronald Reagan explained, there's no better welfare program than getting a job. Letting people keep their money helps everyone. The more money left in the hands of workers, investors, and entrepreneurs—that is, the productive class—the more we all benefit, including the poor. Smaller government and lower taxes create more incentives to work, save, invest, and engage in entrepreneurial endeavors. When the government takes less in taxes and imposes lower regulatory costs, businessmen have more money to hire people. Consumers have more money to spend in those businesses. More people work, and more people prosper. Simple, isn't it?

What the Government Is Costing You

According to the Americans for Tax Reform Foundation:[18]

- The "Cost of Government Day" is the date in the calendar year when the average American worker has earned enough gross income to pay off his or her share of spending and regulatory burdens imposed by all levels of government.

- In 2006, that day was July 12. This means that the average American taxpayer had to work 192.5 days to pay off his or her share of government spending. This was eight more days than in 2000.

- Federal spending grew by 10.2 percent between 2000 and 2006.

- The cost of government consumes about half of the national income.

LIBERAL LUNACY:
"We need high taxes to punish the rich."

"We don't resent people who are doing well," Barack Obama pleaded, just days after issuing an economic plan that called for punishing the wealthy by raising their taxes on dividends and capital gains.[19] Of course, we must assume that Obama is telling the truth here. He doesn't "resent" the rich, he just wants the government to seize their money. Hey, no hard feelings.

Perhaps because so many liberal politicians, such as Ted Kennedy, Howard Dean and John Kerry, were born into or married into wealth, they fail to understand the direct relationship between hard work, saving, and economic success. The demand to punish the rich is especially ironic coming from limousine liberals and radical chic types who ought to be wealthy enough to realize that soaking the rich means punishing everyone. Says a wise and self-made rich man, Rush Limbaugh: "It's easy to talk about punishing wealthy people for their supposed greed. But when you talk about taxing the rich, you're talking about taxing capital. And taxing capital results in damage to more than just the wealthy. In other words, you can't punish the wealthy without also punishing the middle class. That's because the wealthy invest their capital to create new jobs, most of which accrue to those not wealthy."[20] Think of it this way—when Paris Hilton or another Hollywood starlet spends $250,000 on a birthday party, who receives the moola? The waiters, caterers, doormen, and bartenders working the party. Thus, even when a rich starlet spends a fortune on a "frivolous" party, the workers of America directly benefit.

Government policy shouldn't punish the rich for their success; it should instead empower the non-rich to get rich. Conservatives want to make the poor rich, while liberals want to make the rich poor.

Also, where in the name of Joe Stalin did any American ever get the idea that it was the role of our government to punish people for being wealthy—and even to enslave them? Taxation is, after all, a form of slavery. Hyperbolic? Hysterical? I don't think so. What is slavery, anyway? A slave is someone who is owned by another. The slave owner tells the slave what he can and cannot do. Most importantly from the slave owner's perspective, the owner gets to keep not just the slave himself but also the fruits of his labor without having to pay a dime for them.

Today, those of us who pay taxes have become partial slaves to the government. If the government decides that you have to give up 50 percent of your income regardless of whether you want to, you must do so. The government decides how much of the fruits of your labor it will seize. If you refuse to play along, you go to jail.

That modern government engages in activities that enslave us is not just unfortunate; it's inconsistent with the principles of individual freedom upon which our nation was founded. You should be allowed to act as you see fit unless doing so would violate the natural rights of another. Says Leonard Read: "Man either accepts the idea that the Creator is the endower of rights, or he submits to the idea that the state is the endower of rights. I can think of no other alternative."[21]

Those Who Don't Learn From the Past Are Doomed to Repeat It

    Back in the hot summer of 1990, Senate Majority Leader George Mitchell proudly engineered the infamous 'luxury tax,' a nasty little tithe on everything from furs to jewelry to yachts. Democrats were proud: Not only were they throwing new dollars at the Treasury, they'd done it by socking it to the rich. The wealthy, in the words of then House majority leader Dick Gephardt, would finally pay 'their fair share.'

    Within a year, Mr. Mitchell was back in the Senate passionately demanding an end to the same dreaded luxury tax. The levy had devastated his home state of Maine's boatbuilding business, throwing yard workers, managers and salesmen out of jobs. The luxury tax was repealed by 1993. . . .

—*Wall Street Journal*[22]

LIBERAL LUNACY:
"Reagan's tax cuts benefited the rich and hurt ordinary Americans."

Liberals don't really hate Ronald Reagan because they think his tax cuts hurt the poor. Nor do they want high taxes because they care about the poor. They want taxes high so they can have lots of government money on hand, which they can use to create more Democratic voters—voters who depend upon government jobs and subsidies. Democrats need tax revenues to keep government handouts going. After all, Democrats gain power by doling out political goodies. But these goodies cost money—money that has to come from the taxpayer. Cut off the flow of that money and you cut off the Democrats' power.[23] That's why Ronald Reagan was Public Enemy Number One for liberals: by cutting taxes, Reagan threatened the parasitic, unproductive class dependent upon taxpayer-funded government largesse. This threatened the Democrats' political sustenance.

In 1981, Reagan persuaded Congress to enact his 25 percent across-the-board tax cut. It worked: after Reagan's tax cuts the economy grew (accounting for inflation) by 31 percent between 1983 and 1989, for an annual economic growth rate of 3.5 percent. In the process, the Reagan economy created almost 20 million new jobs, doubled the value of the stock market, and reduced both poverty and unemployment rates.[24] In doing so, Reagan showed how less government and lower taxes lead to greater riches for all Americans.

VRWC TALKING POINTS

★ Bush's tax cuts were a tremendous economic boon that benefited all Americans—even the poor who don't pay any taxes.

★ Punishing oil companies by confiscating their profits will only increase the price of oil. The higher oil prices get, the more profitable it becomes for private businesses to develop alternative energy sources.

★ Instead of tinkering with our unmanageable federal tax code, we should consider more comprehensive reforms like the flat tax and the fair tax.

★ Government-built projects and government-provided jobs come at the expense of the taxpayer and the overall economy.

★ The best way for the government to help the poor is to allow the private sector to keep its profits, thereby creating new jobs for them.

★ The government should encourage the poor to get rich, not punish the rich for their success through confiscatory taxation.

★ Reagan's tax cuts were an economic success. Liberals opposed his tax policy because it threatened their parasitic constituency that relies on government funding.

INTRUSIVENESS OF GOVERNMENT: WELCOME TO THE NANNY STATE

"Give me liberty or give me death," proclaimed Patrick Henry. It's hard to argue that we're following his motto today, when we live under a government that regulates everything from what we can eat to how our toilets work. Liberals claim all these regulations are for our own good. When will they learn that the best thing the government can do for us is to let us live freely?

★ ★ ★ ★ ★

LIBERAL LUNACY:
"The government should strictly regulate campaign financing due to the corrupting influence of money on politics."

First of all, how exactly does money "corrupt" the political process? If I support some candidate, how is it "corrupt" for me to donate money to help his campaign? If a zillionaire like Michael Bloomberg wants to run for president, he can use as much of his own money as he wants, but if poor ol' Joe Sixpack runs for office, why can't rich supporters toss him or his party a few million to assist his efforts?

The truth is, campaign finance "reform" is a farce. It's just another attempt to empower government regulators at the expense of the people, telling us how we can and cannot spend our money. The increasing regulation of political contributions to parties and candidates hasn't even done anything to eliminate money from politics—big contributors are simply switching their donations from the parties and candidates to special interest groups like political action committees (PACs) and 527 organizations. George Soros, one of the liberals' chief financiers, is a great example. He spent close to $18 million lobbying for campaign finance reform. Then, after the adoption of the McCain-Feingold law put new limits on contributions to parties, Soros donated tens of millions of dollars to moveon.org and other liberal PACs and 527 groups.[1] Soros obviously wants to keep his own money in the system—it's everyone else's money that he's trying to eliminate.

And it's not just money that the bureaucrats are looking to regulate; it's speech too. The McCain-Feingold bill expressly banned various kinds of organizations from running radio or TV ads that mention a candidate shortly before a primary or election. Liberal, mainstream newspapers like the *New York Times* were all in favor of these restrictions because the rules didn't apply to them. Their editorials could continue flacking for liberal issues and leftwing candidates, while grassroots citizens' groups were silenced. Thankfully, in June 2007, the Supreme Court considerably loosened these restrictions, which really should be struck down altogether.

Liberals decry as "censors" anyone who questions whether taxpayers should be forced to subsidize the most

obscene art imaginable, like images of Robert Mapple-
thorpe putting whips where they're not designed to go.
But when it comes to core political speech—the exact
kind protected by the First Amendment—they insist that
we need speech police to keep citizens from joining together to criticize political candidates. Their viewpoint
is pretty straightforward: "Free speech for me, not for
thee."

LIBERAL LUNACY:
"We need the government to regulate
our health."

Liberals are desperately trying to seize control of our lives
by regulating our health. For example, John Edwards brags
that his universal health care scheme would *require* Americans to get preventive care.[2] Do you really want John Edwards telling you how often you *must* see the doctor? The
controlling impulse underlying this kind of socialized
(read: government-controlled) health care was evident in
a 2007 policy recommendation by British *conservatives*.
(Clearly, the British Right has fallen a long way since
Churchill and Thatcher). That proposal seeks to deny various treatments to people whose lifestyles, according to
government standards, are unhealthy.[3]

Can you imagine the conversations with your insurer
under that kind of system? "Gee, Mr. Smith, I can see you
really need a bypass, but I'm afraid you exceeded the
allowable number of bags of potato chips last year. What's
more, you only worked out for half the year. Sorry, but
your request for a bypass is denied. Try drinking some
green tea instead. Next!"

Nanny state health regulators are easy to find below the federal level as well. In fact, local and state governments are often the worst offenders, sticking the government's regulating snout into the minutest areas of our lives.

Take smoking bans. Innumerable cities and even entire states have banned smoking in public buildings, including restaurants and bars. What gives some bureaucrat the right to tell the owner of a restaurant that his customers can't smoke in his own establishment? If customers don't want to be around smoke, there's an ingenious alternative to outlawing smoking—they can choose to eat at non-smoking restaurants. But anti-smoking laws are needed to defend the health of the wait staff, the regulators insist, as if waiters don't have the mental capabilities to weigh the risks and choose whether or not to work at a smoking restaurant.

Unsurprisingly, the Democrats' Nanny-in-Chief, Hillary Clinton, is a die-hard supporter of smoking bans. She brags that New York's restaurants have increased business since the city's smoking ban took effect.[4] And liberals accuse us conservatives of prioritizing profits over civil liberties. . . .

Since these bureaucrats have decided that we can't smoke in restaurants, it's only natural that they begin dictating to us what we can and cannot eat. In December 2006, ultra-liberal New York City banned the use of trans fats in restaurants because they're unhealthy. Well, what if we want trans fats anyway? What if we want to suck down a slew of trans fats and finish it off with a nice cigarette? Is hunting down and punishing these kinds of "offenders" really the best use of police resources?

Once nanny state liberals seize the power to impose their personal health standards on us, there's no logical end to their regulatory zeal. It's only a matter of time before smoking and trans fats are banned in private residences. We saw the first step in this direction in October 2007, when the city council in Belmont, California outlawed smoking in most private apartments.[5] Liberals have embraced a strange new form of Puritanism, wielding the power of the state to insist that everyone embrace their notion of a healthy lifestyle. (And let's face it—how healthy can incense, marijuana, and patchouli really be?) We're going to be healthy whether we want to or not, it seems—or we'll face the legal consequences.

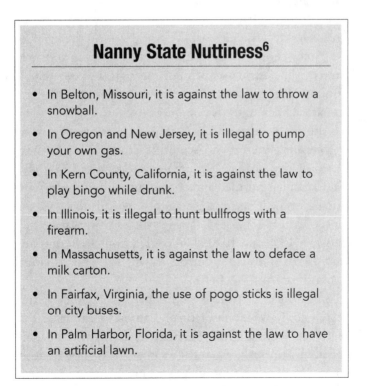

Nanny State Nuttiness[6]

- In Belton, Missouri, it is against the law to throw a snowball.
- In Oregon and New Jersey, it is illegal to pump your own gas.
- In Kern County, California, it is against the law to play bingo while drunk.
- In Illinois, it is illegal to hunt bullfrogs with a firearm.
- In Massachusetts, it is against the law to deface a milk carton.
- In Fairfax, Virginia, the use of pogo sticks is illegal on city buses.
- In Palm Harbor, Florida, it is against the law to have an artificial lawn.

LIBERAL LUNACY:
"We're heading for Armageddon unless the government halts global warming."

If it pays for liberals to use public health as an excuse to expand the reach of government, then global warming is their big government jackpot. Global warming is a political crusade and a religion wrapped into one. It's also a lifestyle choice. And most importantly, unlike vegetarianism and other entertaining leftwing fetishes, it's a lifestyle choice that has to be forced onto everyone.

Liberals really love doomsday scenarios precisely because they can so easily be used to expand the scope of government intrusion. Over the past few decades, the greens have warned us that the world was on the brink of destruction due to overpopulation, declining food resources, the destruction of the rainforests, and even global cooling. When the earth refuses to cooperate with their scenarios, liberals just break out a new one.

Although the earth has gotten slightly warmer in the last century, there is no scientific consensus as to how much of that change—if any—is due to human activity. The earth has warmed and cooled throughout history, inducing everything from ice ages to periods that were, in fact, warmer than today. Recently, the earth warmed up between 1895 and 1940, then cooled from 1940 until the mid-1970s. This latter period spawned the bogus global cooling panic of the 1970s.[7]

Since the 1970s, the earth has been in another warming trend. How much of this is caused by humans? The truth is, we don't know. The trend may simply be part of the earth's normal long-term weather fluctuation. Indeed, some scientists question whether human-induced climate change is even possible. One of these skeptics is Canadian

2000 Presidential Election Electoral Vote

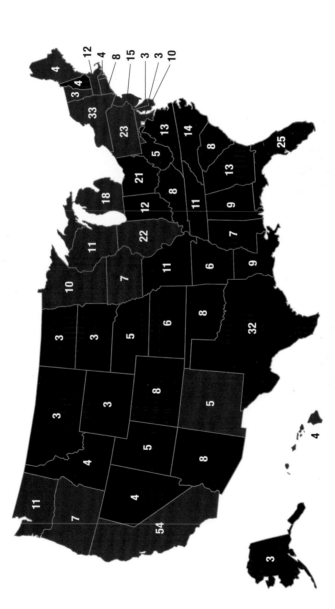

■ Bush (271)
■ Gore (266)
270 needed to win

2004 Presidential Election Electoral Vote

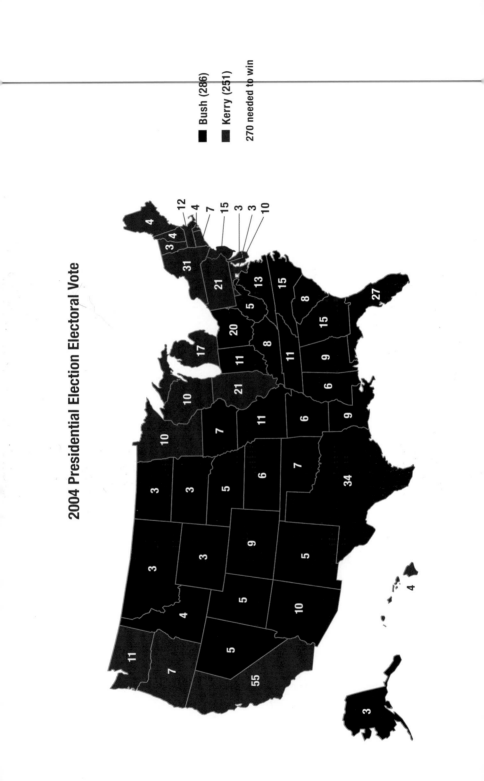

■ Bush (286)

■ Kerry (251)

270 needed to win

2004 Presidential Election

Level of Support by State

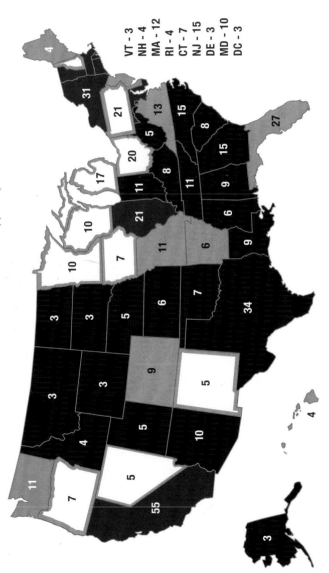

VT - 3
NH - 4
MA - 12
RI - 4
CT - 7
NJ - 15
DE - 3
MD - 10
DC - 3

Strong Kerry (146)

Weak Kerry (37)

Barely Kerry (69)

Exactly tied (0)

Barely Bush (37)

Weak Bush (66)

Strong Bush (183)

Needed to win: 270

Source: www.electoral-vote.com/evp2004/index.html

Current Map of the Senate

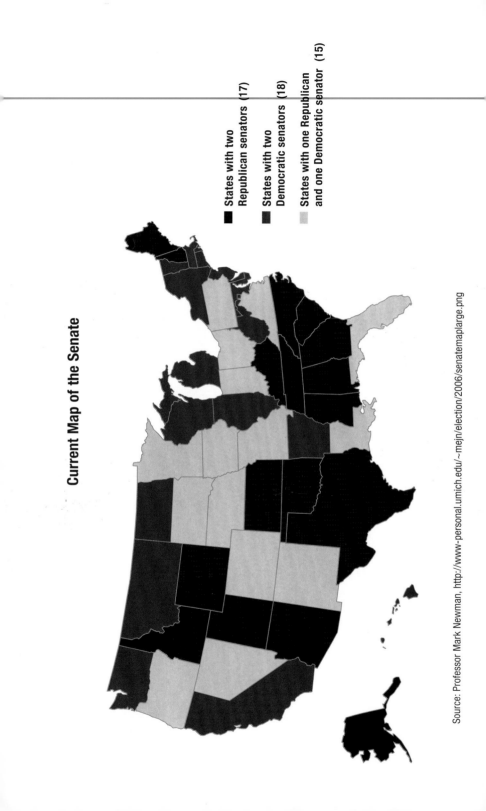

■ States with two Republican senators (17)

■ States with two Democratic senators (18)

■ States with one Republican and one Democratic senator (15)

Source: Professor Mark Newman, http://www-personal.umich.edu/~mejn/election/2006/senatemaplarge.png

2008 Senate Election

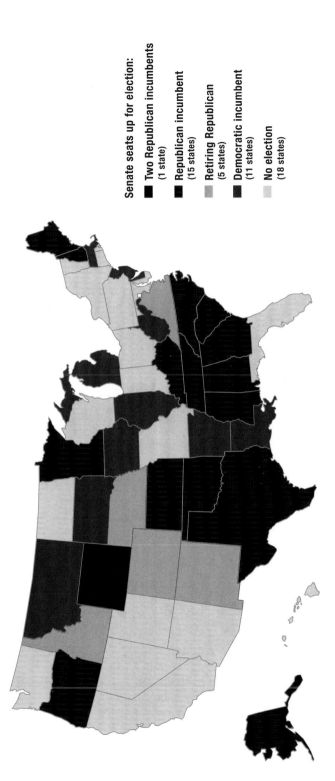

Senate seats up for election:

■ Two Republican incumbents
(1 state)

■ Republican incumbent
(15 states)

▨ Retiring Republican
(5 states)

■ Democratic incumbent
(11 states)

☐ No election
(18 states)

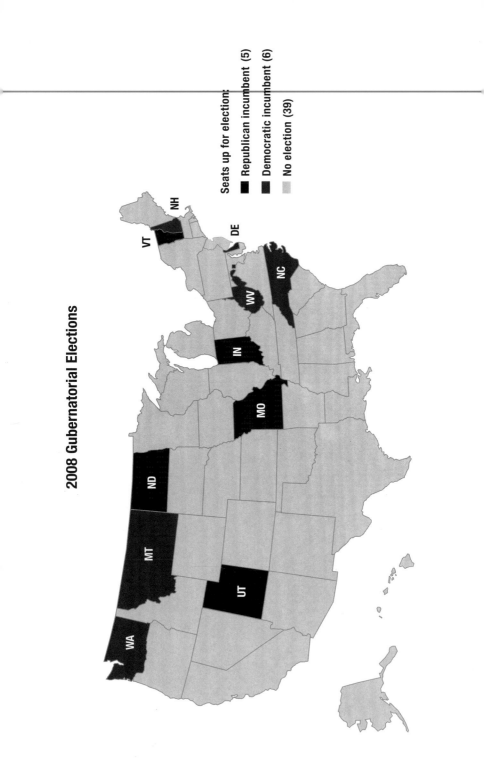

2008 Gubernatorial Elections

Seats up for election:

- Republican incumbent (5)
- Democratic incumbent (6)
- No election (39)

Current Party Control of State Legislatures

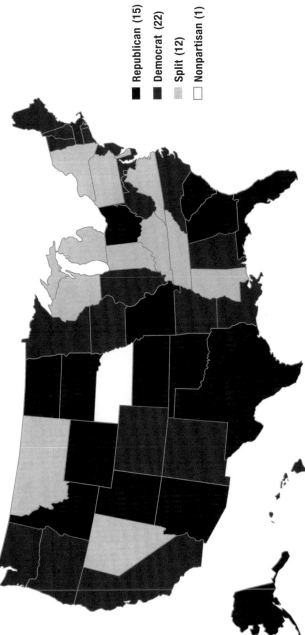

- ■ Republican (15)
- ■ Democrat (22)
- ▨ Split (12)
- □ Nonpartisan (1)

Anti-Affirmative Action Ballot Initiatives

The American Civil Rights Coalition (ACRC) has successfully organized anti-affirmative action ballot initiatives in three states. These initiatives prohibited the state governments and public institutions from granting preferential treatment based on race or gender. The following map shows the three states that passed ACRC-sponsored initiatives, as well as the five states in which the ACRC is currently working to get similar initiatives placed on the ballot for the 2008 elections.

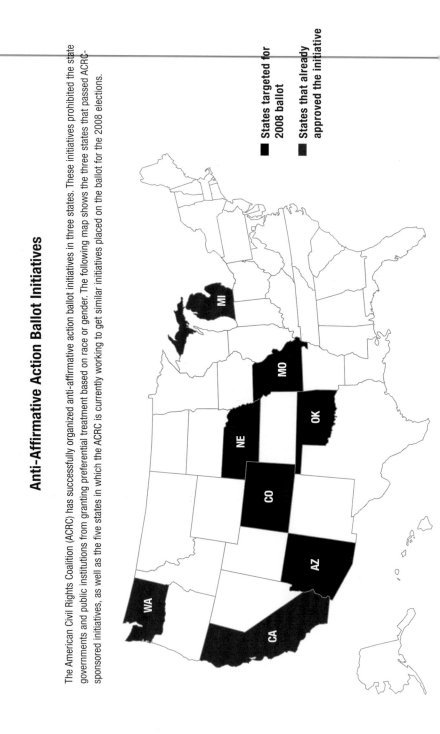

■ States targeted for 2008 ballot

■ States that already approved the initiative

climatologist Timothy Ball, who has labeled the global warming scare "the greatest deception in the history of science."[8] Nevertheless, liberals simply assert that temperature change *must* be due to humans, and that we'd better mend our ways before we all go the way of the dinosaurs.

As Chris Horner notes, there's a big lie at the heart of the climate change hysteria—"catastrophic manmade global warming" is neither catastrophic, nor manmade, nor global. Here's the breakdown: Firstly, it's not catastrophic— the likely consequences of the planet warming up by a few degrees do not include massive droughts, flooding, or famines, as global warming alarmists insist. In fact, the negative aspects of a slightly warmer planet are minor and will probably be offset by the benefits that warmer weather will bring to sectors like agriculture and forestry. Secondly, it's not manmade—or at least, there's no definitive proof for this claim, as noted above. And finally, it's not global— while some parts of the earth are heating up, temperatures in other parts, like most of the southern hemisphere, are unchanged or actually cooling.[9]

But mere science is not going to stand in the way of a good environmental crusade. Liberals will attribute every weather fluctuation, environmental trend, and international dispute to global warming. Is it hot out? It's global warming! Is it *cold* out? It's global warming![10] Is there international tension over disputed land? It's global warming![11] When wildfires tore through southern California in October 2007, what did Democratic senator Harry Reid blame it on? You guessed it—global warming. Unfortunately for Reid, his suggestion came just days before federal investigators found that much of the fire was due to arson.[12]

The demands for regulation to fight climate change are so drastic that it's no exaggeration to describe global warming as a new totalitarian creed. The new regulations on industry demanded by the Kyoto accord would have cost the U.S. an estimated $325 billion, according to Yale University's William Nordhaus and Joseph Boyer. Although the U.S. Senate rightfully rejected such an outrageous burden on the U.S. economy, the demands just keep on coming, growing more preposterous all the time.

TerraPass Inc., a California company that promotes alternative energy, proposed eliminating dryers and returning to clotheslines.[13] Fossil fuel pollution expert Gregg Marland suggested replacing every fossil-fuel-powered electricity plant in the world with windmills, solar panels, and nuclear power plants.[14] Not to be outdone, John Guillebaud, co-chairman of the British environmental thinktank Optimum Population Trust, admonished that couples should have no more than two children due to the harmful carbon dioxide output of every human being.[15] Pop star Sheryl Crow chimed in with the, er, uncomfortable proposal to limit the use of toilet paper to one square per sitting.[16]

A Scientific Consensus: Al Gore Is Annoying

❝ Without energy, life is brutal and short. So, I don't see very much effect in trying to scare people into not using energy, when it is the very basis of how we can live in our society. . . . The climate is so difficult to understand, Mother Nature is so complex, and so the uncertainties are great, and then to hear [Al Gore] speak with such certainty and such confidence about what the climate is going to do is—well, I suppose I could be kind and say, it's annoying to me. ❞

—John Christy, member of the Intergovernmental Panel on Climate Change, which shared the 2007 Nobel Peace Prize with Al Gore.[17]

It's no surprise that Al Gore has jumped on the global warming bandwagon. The benefits for him go far beyond the "honor" of joining the likes of Yassir Arafat as a Nobel Peace prize winner. Denied the presidency by American voters, he's adopted a cause that stands to provide him with even more power over our everyday lives.

> **CONSERVATIVES SAY IT BEST**
>
> " Never, other than during the two world wars, has there been such a concerted effort by opinion-forming institutions to indoctrinate Americans. "
>
> —George Will, on the campaign to spread awareness of global warming[18]

LIBERAL LUNACY:
"We need government regulations for our own safety."

Yeah, right. We need government regulations to fine barbers for having "too much hair on the floor." To prevent the late Mother Teresa from building a homeless shelter in New York. To require banks to install Braille keypads on drive-through ATMs. To punish farmers for shooting bears in self-defense. To fine casket salesmen for selling their wares without an embalmer's license.

Government bureaucrats—America's unelected royal elite—are running amok and declaring war on ordinary Americans and their businesses. It's time to call a halt. Want to do something that is not regulated by the government? Forget it. Government regulations apply to housing, banking, recreational activities, land use, occupations, and even using the toilet. That's right: under a 1992 federal law, toilets installed in American homes must be limited to 1.6 gallons per flush; showerheads must limit water usage to 2.5 gallons per minute.

I say let's fire the government toilet inspectors and use the money to beef up a few anti-terrorism units—or give it back to the taxpayer. These nit-picking regulations not only limit our freedoms, they don't even accomplish what they're supposed to.

After all, half of all violations of Occupational Health and Safety Agency (OSHA) regulations don't come from real threats to health and safety, but—horror of horrors—from failure to maintain proper paperwork![19] Quick—call the file cabinet police! OSHA employs over 2,300 people; its 1,000 inspectors visited work sites 36,000 times in 2001 alone, discovering almost 80,000 safety violations. These resulted in fines of $82 million.[20] Feel safer yet? Not so fast: one recent study shows that "increased safety regulation actually *increases* the occupational death rate."[21] Another estimates that the current regulatory system is actually responsible for as many as 60,000 deaths every year.[22]

Hard to believe? It shouldn't be. Billions of dollars are squandered on eliminating negligible or nonexistent risks, while you remain unprotected from other, more serious ones.

Take the Corporate Average Fuel Economy (CAFE) standards for cars. The direct result of federal fuel economy laws was the manufacture of smaller, more fuel-efficient cars. There was just one catch: these nifty new gas-efficient beauties were much more likely to get flattened in an accident than the old gas-guzzlers were. The former head of the National Highway Traffic Safety Administration, Jerry Ralph Curry, reports, "since CAFE legislation took effect, more people have been killed because of it than died in Vietnam."[23] Maybe the liberals should turn their "no blood for oil" slogan on the federal bureaucrats who run their beloved regulatory agencies.

Now excuse me while I go refuel my Land Rover.

LIBERAL LUNACY:
"We need government regulations to protect small businesses."

Without government regulations, say the liberals, pretty soon Wal-Mart and Staples will run the last mom-and-pop store out of business, and Mom and Pop will be eating watery soup with plastic spoons down at the homeless shelter. But in fact, regulations saddle small businesses with gigantic costs and mountains of red tape—so much that it all amounts to a serious threat to the survival of small- and medium-sized businesses, which create two out of every three new jobs in the U.S.[24] The Small Business Administration estimates that small businesses have to pay $5,000 for each employee every year just to keep up with the niggling rules and mountains of paperwork that the government requires.[25]

If employers were freed from all these regulations, they could pay their employees more or expand their businesses. But as it is, small businesses are strangled by red tape.

LIBERAL LUNACY:
"We need regulation to rein in shady businesses and discourage scofflaws."

Liberals seem to think that if they create minute regulations covering every aspect of business and life, outlaws will turn in their guns and peace will reign in the land. Nobody will be bilked or defrauded, nobody will be conned by hucksters. But these volumes and volumes of legal codes don't really make us any more honest. In fact, regulations are just another form of taxation. They're just another way for the government to exercise control over us.

In 2004, the total cost to the economy of all regulation was estimated to be $877 billion. This is a hidden tax of more than $8,000 per year per American family and equal to about 43 percent of the entire federal spending budget.[26] Today, the costs of the federal regulatory burden has been estimated at $750—$860 billion a year, or almost $10,000 for every American household. Add in state and local regulatory costs, and the burden leaps to $20,000 per household.[27]

The rules are so many and so minute that they're turning us into a nation of lawbreakers. The documents upon which this country was founded—the Constitution, Bill of Rights, and Declaration of Independence—are all short and to the point. In stark contrast, the Code of Federal Regulations is about 75,000 pages long. It takes up twenty feet of bookshelf space—and that doesn't include statutes or state and local regulations. The U.S. General Accounting Office (GAO) says that between April 1, 1996, and December 31, 1997, federal regulatory agencies issued almost 7,000 final rules and sent them to Congress for review; Congress approved them all.[28]

Meanwhile, there are about sixty federal regulatory agencies that exist only to enforce these laws. The sheer volume of regulations makes the law virtually unknowable. Also, regulations are often so ambiguous that you need an army of lawyers just to tell you what they mean. All in all, it makes for a situation in which you are most likely, at this very moment, somehow breaking the law.

The most shameful example of this is the tax code. Tax laws are so complex and unreadable that businessmen and families order their financial affairs only with great difficulty. Many must take on the additional expense of hiring professional tax preparers. Every year, Americans spend over 4.6 billion hours at a cost of $140 billion just to comply with the federal tax code and regulations.[29] The result is fewer success stories and fewer businesses in general. When laws are unpredictable, people are less willing to take risks because they can't predict the outcomes of their actions.

You want honesty? Deregulate. In 1997, the White House Office of Management and Budget (OMB) admitted that higher prices and inefficient operations are the direct result of stifling regulations. Regulations even discourage entrepreneurs from starting new businesses. It's

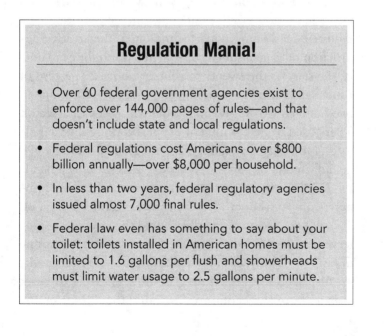

Regulation Mania!

- Over 60 federal government agencies exist to enforce over 144,000 pages of rules—and that doesn't include state and local regulations.

- Federal regulations cost Americans over $800 billion annually—over $8,000 per household.

- In less than two years, federal regulatory agencies issued almost 7,000 final rules.

- Federal law even has something to say about your toilet: toilets installed in American homes must be limited to 1.6 gallons per flush and showerheads must limit water usage to 2.5 gallons per minute.

time to let a businessman make an honest buck without making him jump through a dizzying array of government hoops. When government relaxes control, Americans prosper. The proof is out there—over the past twenty years, Americans have reaped the benefits of the deregulation of the transportation, natural gas, and other industries. Experience shows that the profit motive is the best basis for decision-making: the decision maker faces consequences of his own making. Regulators have no such discipline.

LIBERAL LUNACY:
"Government must regulate the economy because free markets create unemployment."

In a certain sense, it's true. Free market economies commit "creative destruction";[30] they eliminate old industries and jobs but, in the process, create new ones. By creating new industries and laborsaving technologies, the creative destruction of capitalism creates a better world for everyone. At the start of the twentieth century, about 25 percent of Americans worked in agriculture. Now, only about one in two hundred workers is employed in the agricultural sector. There used to be 1.4 million people working on the railroads. Now there are about 200,000. There used to be 400 manufacturers of automobiles. Now there is only a handful. IBM was once considered the great American computer company, but in 1993 the company almost went bust.

Are these disasters? Hardly. Should the government intervene to "save" dying industries? No way. Whenever one industry is destroyed, a new industry is born. Those workers displaced in one industry are now available to work elsewhere in the economy. Certainly the advent of the automobile destroyed lots of jobs in the buggy whip factories, but the rise of the car helped the entire society become more mobile—while simultaneously creating thousands of new jobs making and servicing cars. Liberals fail to understand that an essential (and desirable) part of any capitalist economy is the destruction of jobs—manufacturing jobs in particular. But at the same time, laborsaving devices create more and better jobs while also raising standards of living.

Want full employment in America right now? Ban the use of tractors. How many jobs have been lost in farming over the last 100–150 years due to the advent of the tractor? If these farming jobs had not been destroyed by tractors, then food today would not be as cheap and plentiful—and many of us who now work in air-conditioned office buildings fighting with copy machines would find ourselves sweating in the hot sun harvesting crops. We'd all have jobs, but would you really opt for full employment under such circumstances?

Of course, the recognized societal benefits from free markets do come with a cost. Those who lose their jobs in old, dying industries obviously suffer. However, they too benefit from the cheaper and more plentiful products made available by the new advances that eliminated their jobs. And, they can seek new employment in the new industries that have been created in the process.

VRWC TALKING POINTS

★ Campaign finance reform has not only utterly failed to remove "big money" from politics, but it has also resulted in the adoption of unconstitutional limits on core free speech.

★ Liberals are using their supposed concern for our health as an excuse to expand dramatically the reach of government into our daily lives.

★ The global warming scare is the liberals' big government jackpot—a supposed threat to the entire planet that requires a historic level of government regulation to solve.

★ Government safety regulations are unnecessary, often ineffective, and sometimes even make us less safe.

★ Government regulations are a burden for small businesses, not a benefit.

★ Government regulations on business represent a hidden tax on Americans that stifles economic freedom.

★ In a free market, old industries naturally die out as technology advances. The government cannot, and should not try to, interfere with this process.

THE IRAQ WAR: SURRENDER IS NOT A WINNING STRATEGY

Liberals' solution to the Iraq War is to cut and run, leaving behind a bloodbath they can blame on President Bush. With their affinity for surrendering, it's surprising they haven't moved to France.

* * * * *

LIBERAL LUNACY:
"Terrorists are primarily motivated by the Iraq War. If we withdraw from Iraq, terrorists will stop attacking us."

Terrorists were attacking us long before we began fighting in Iraq. The USS *Cole* bombing, the African embassy bombings, the Khobar Towers bombing, and of course, the September 11 attacks all pre-dated our invasion of Iraq. It's true that terrorists are now traveling to Iraq to attack U.S. forces. But there's no reason to believe that if we withdrew tomorrow the terrorists would happily return home and abandon the jihad. Without Iraq as the central focus of the War on Terror, the terrorists would simply find other places to attack us—like in America itself.

Liberals like to portray Iraq as a completely separate issue from the War on Terror. They can't admit that Iraq is the primary battlefield where a larger war is playing out. They think we can just pull up stakes from Iraq and go home with no consequences other than earning the good will of the terrorists.

In fact, if we withdrew from Iraq, the most likely scenario is that the country would either turn into a terrorist state controlled by Iran and Syria, or would collapse into anarchy and become a safe haven for international jihadists. Iran and Syria fully understand the stakes in Iraq—if the U.S. were to succeed in stabilizing a democratic government there, it would embolden democratic reformers in their own countries and could threaten their regimes. A sudden U.S. withdrawal from Iraq, however, would allow both countries to expand their influence into Iraq and possibly even control it through a proxy regime.

A cut-and-run strategy is to terrorists what blood in the water is to sharks—a reason to attack. A withdrawal from Iraq would reinvigorate terrorists everywhere, who would see that America lacks the determination to confront them. It would send the unmistakable message that the U.S. can no longer stand to bear casualties in its own defense. Our allies throughout the world would view us, as Osama bin Laden does, as a "paper tiger" and then shift their allegiances to our enemies.

According to the liberal worldview, wars only stem from misunderstandings that can always be resolved if we just show more compassion to our enemies, hold their hands, and sing "Kumbaya" together. But in fact, the world is a treacherous place where most governments will ally with whatever state can further their interests. And it's rare that allying with a weak, irresolute, defeated state will further a

According to senior U.S. administration and military officials, Iran, assisted by Syria, is taking the following actions in order to sabotage Iraqi democracy:[1]

- Forging ties with al Qaeda elements and Sunni Arab militias in Iraq

- Directing rocket attacks against U.S. and British forces in Iraq

- Supplying weapons to terrorist groups and training them in Iran

- Expanding contacts with paramilitary forces in Iraq and with Kurdish parties, including U.S. allies such as the Patriotic Union of Kurdistan

- Planning to orchestrate a nationwide offensive against coalition forces by al Qaeda, Sunni insurgents, and Shi'ite militias in hopes of "trigger[ing] a political mutiny in Washington and a U.S. retreat."

nation's interests. Ultimately, we are much more likely to attain peace and maintain solid alliances through a policy of strength, determination, and military victory than by seeking to appease our enemies by embracing defeat.

LIBERAL LUNACY:
"We should withdraw from Iraq because it has become a civil war."

The fighting in Iraq has surely taken on some features of a civil war, as Iraqi Shi'ites and Sunnis square off throughout the country. But what's so special about a civil war? It would seem that, to liberals, if the terrorists in Iraq were united in attacking U.S. troops, then we could continue the fight. But because the terrorists often attack each other and other Iraqis, we shouldn't be involved—we're "taking sides in a civil war!"

Of course, it would be best if there were no terrorism in Iraq at all. But if there is terrorism, a civil war is a better situation for us than if the terrorists unify all their efforts against our troops. It's easier to defeat our enemy—the terrorists—if they're first divided. "Divide and conquer" is a pretty well-established military strategy, but apparently liberals don't learn it in their peace studies seminars.

Additionally, liberals cheered when "their" president, Bill Clinton, sent the U.S. military to intervene in all kinds of civil strife in Bosnia, Kosovo, Somalia, and Haiti. In fact, sending troops to end the civil war in Sudan has become a popular pet cause of the Left. So liberals obviously don't even believe their own argument that becoming involved in a civil war is either immoral or unwinnable. Their real viewpoint is that we can only take sides in a civil war when there's a liberal president sending troops into a situation where there is no vital U.S. interest at stake. For liberals, the lack of a national interest proves our selflessness. They want to see the U.S. military turned into a kind of global charity service. But in a place like Iraq, where the consequences of defeat would be catastrophic for America—oh no, we can't continue fighting there; it's a "civil war."

LIBERAL LUNACY:
"Iraq is another Vietnam."

A simple look at the casualty figures reveals how inappropriate the comparison is between the Iraq and Vietnam wars. The U.S. lost approximately 58,000 men in Vietnam, compared to around 4,000 men in Iraq. That's right—our total losses in Iraq are around 7 *percent* of those from Vietnam. While the loss of every U.S. serviceman's life is tragic, we need to keep a little perspective when we hear overheated comparisons of the present conflict to Vietnam.

One comparison between Iraq and Vietnam, however, is valid: the consequences of a U.S. defeat. If we withdraw, what will happen to our allies in Iraq, or even the average Iraqi who doesn't support the jihadists' program? The lesson of Vietnam is instructive here. After we left Vietnam, the south fell to the communists. With no countervailing force left in the region, Cambodia and Laos quickly succumbed to the communists as well. The result was a humanitarian tragedy that liberals don't like to talk about—the establishment of murderous "re-education" camps and a massive wave of refugees, or "boat people." In Cambodia alone, the genocidal communists of the Khmer Rouge slaughtered an estimated 1.7 million of their own countrymen. And the liberals, our great humanitarians, didn't lift a finger to help them. They had finally secured a great victory for themselves—our defeat in Vietnam—and they couldn't care less about the tragic consequences.

LIBERAL LUNACY:
"At the very least, we need a timetable to withdraw from Iraq."

Rushing the troops home without regard to the consequences is not only a bad idea, but a dangerous one. Why would we go to war and then refuse to give the troops enough time to accomplish their mission—no matter how long it takes? We stationed U.S. troops in Europe for fifty years during the Cold War to serve as a deterrent to the Soviets, and we've had troops in South Korea since the Korean War.

There should be no artificial timetable for withdrawing U.S. troops from any military conflicts including the Iraq War. Even Independent-Democratic senator Joe Lieberman opposes doing so, arguing it would "discourage our troops because it seems to be heading for the door. It will encourage the terrorists, it will confuse the Iraqi people."[2] What war has ever been won on a timetable? On December 7, 1941, did FDR propose a timetable for winning World War II? Hardly—he just proposed winning! Who cares what a bunch of suit-and-tie politicians sitting in air-conditioned offices in Washington, D.C., think must occur in Iraq? Decisions about troop levels and military strategy should be made by military commanders, not by artificial timetables set by politicians. As President Bush explained, "setting an artificial deadline to withdraw would vindicate the terrorists' tactics of beheadings and suicide bombings and mass murder—and invite new attacks on America."[3]

Liberals may also have an ulterior motive for wanting to rush our troops out of Iraq—a U.S. victory there would be harmful to the Democrats. Don't take my word for it—take the word of Democratic congressman James Clyburn, the House majority whip. When asked how he'd react if General Petraeus reported to Congress that the surge strategy was working in Iraq (which is exactly what Petraeus reported), Clyburn replied, "Well, that would be a real big problem for us, no question about that."[4]

Yes, U.S. military victory is a "real big problem" for the Democrats. Ensuring a U.S. defeat in Iraq is the most important foreign policy objective for their base (aside from deporting Dick Cheney to Papua New Guinea). If the surge remains effective, the Democrats will lose their biggest issue to rally their supporters to the polls.

How unhinged are the Democrats over the war issue? Here's what Democratic congressman Pete Stark said to congressional Republicans about the war: "You don't have money to fund the war, or children. But you're going to spend it to blow up innocent people if we can get enough kids to grow old enough for you to send to Iraq to get their heads blown off for the president's amusement."[5]

Michelle Malkin's response could apply to the entire Democratic base that applauded Stark's diatribe: "Don't question his patriotism. Question his sanity."[6]

LIBERAL LUNACY:
"The Iraq War is illegal because the UN did not approve it."

The UN is not a collection of free nations; it represents *governments*, not people. A government can be as tyrannical and murderous as it wants and still have a voice in the UN. The genocidal Sudanese government, Castro's communists in Cuba, the mad mullahs in Iran, and North Korea's bizarre Stalinists are all members of the UN. Should we really allow these kinds of governments to tell us how to conduct our international affairs?

The truth is, the UN is a perpetually dysfunctional organization that governments use in pursuit of their own interests. The UN General Assembly is a great example. The General Assembly is a collection of governments with essentially two goals: restraining American power and denouncing Israel. It regularly invites such luminaries as aspiring Venezuelan dictator Hugo Chavez to address its members and blame all the world's problems on America, Israel, and George Bush (or "the devil," as Chavez called him during his 2005 UN speech). The General Assembly has also repeatedly hosted Iranian President Mahmoud Ahmadinejad, whose anti-Western ravings and nuclear ambitions have made him an international outcast everywhere except in American academia (where Columbia welcomed him as a speaker in September 2007). Not much has changed at the UN since 1974, when the General Assembly allowed arch-terrorist Yasser Arafat to deliver an anti-Israel diatribe to its members with a gun strapped to his hip.

Just look at the former UN Commission on Human Rights, whose members included Communist China and Cuba, the Islamic supremacists of Saudi Arabia, and the mass murderers of Sudan. In 2003, Libya, that paragon of human rights, was elected chairman of the commission. The commission became so discredited by its obsession with denouncing Israel that it was abolished and replaced in 2006 with the UN Human Rights Council. The new council took up right where its predecessor left off. Aside from a few weak condemnations of the killers running Sudan and Myanmar, the "renewed" council has not singled out any nation for censure other than Israel, which it has denounced fourteen times.[7]

The UN Security Council has the power to approve actions like the invasion of Iraq. But here, the power to veto U.S. actions is held by countries like China, Russia, and France. To say that all three of these countries have a history of trying to sabotage U.S. foreign policy would be the understatement of the year. China hopes to invade U.S.-allied Taiwan and is the main ally of North Korea; Russia is the key supplier for Iran's nuclear program; and

France is, well, France. Liberal notions that we must gain the approval of our rivals for the conduct of our international affairs are patently absurd. The U.S. Constitution vests the power to declare war in the U.S. Congress, not the UN Security Council. The U.S. military is responsible only to the U.S. president, not to some romanticized world government like the UN.

There is only one word to describe the effort to cede our most vital national powers to the United Nations: un-American.

LIBERAL LUNACY:
"Anyone who supports a war and doesn't actually fight on the frontlines is a chickenhawk."

Funny that we didn't hear liberals trotting out this argument when they supported Bill Clinton's military interventions in Kosovo, Somalia, and Haiti. Apparently, anyone who supports "their" wars is a high-minded, responsible world citizen, while those who support wars they don't like are cowardly chickenhawks.

Let's analyze the reasoning here. Liberals say that only those who serve or have served in combat have the moral authority to support a war. According to this line of reasoning, the vast majority of Americans have no moral right to support U.S. military action anywhere, at any time. So liberals, who are so suspicious of the military that they ban ROTC programs from universities, suddenly morph into military absolutists when they argue about who has a right to support a war.

Liberals claim to champion "victims of discrimination" like disabled people and homosexuals. But since neither of these groups is allowed to fight on the frontlines, according to the chickenhawk argument, none of these subjects of liberal compassion has any moral right to support a war. One should also note that if the chickenhawk argument is correct, then President Clinton lacked the moral authority to send our troops to fight anywhere, since he never saw any combat. (Sorry, his fights with Hillary don't qualify.) And can anyone really argue that presidents Lincoln and Franklin Roosevelt, who also lacked military experience, had no moral authority to fight the Civil War and World War II, respectively?

Why exactly does someone need to experience combat before he can have a legitimate opinion on the need to fight our enemies? Does a man need to go arrest criminals himself in order to support the mission of the police? Does a woman need to grab a hose and fight fires before she has the moral right to support the fire department? The U.S. military exists to defend the country, and every American citizen has the right to support any action he believes will serve that mission. The chickenhawk canard is really just an attempt by liberals to win an argument by smearing their opponents as immoral cowards lacking a legitimate point of view.

LIBERAL LUNACY:
"The mission in Iraq is hideously expensive."

Funny how tax-and-spend liberals suddenly become parsimonious cost-cutters when it comes to defending America. But in this post–September 11 era, the costs of our occupation of Iraq can't be looked at with a dollars-and-cents mentality. Whatever it costs to protect our freedoms, it's a bargain.

The real question is: What would the costs be if we left Iraq? The September 11 attacks probably cost us at least $95 billion. New York City spent almost $5 billion just to clean up Ground Zero. Now, how much more would it cost us if a suicide bomber attacked a nuclear power plant in the U.S., or if a terrorist used a nuclear device in any major city?

The mission in Iraq must be regarded as an investment in the Middle East—an opportunity to create a powerful ally where the seeds of democracy can be planted. Ultimately, the money we spend in Iraq will give the U.S. a toehold in the Middle East and help us shape its future. To some extent, it's already working: Libyan strongman Muammar Gaddafi admitted that the invasion of Iraq convinced him to abandon his WMD programs. How much is that worth, compared to the cost of a Libyan nuke hitting Washington?

LIBERAL LUNACY:
"Wars never solve anything."

From Haight-Ashbury to Greenwich Village, from UC-Berkeley to Harvard Yard, the cry resounds: "Oh, if only we had given peace a chance!" War, they tell us, is never the answer—not in Iraq, not anywhere.

Is that so? Let's see. Six hundred thousand Americans died in the Civil War. A total of 50 million people died in World War II. But the question isn't, "Did lots of people die?" The question is, "Did these wars make any positive difference?"

Well, the Civil War eliminated slavery. Four million African American slaves became free citizens. Was war justified to free the slaves? Are Europe and Asia better off today with the defeat of Nazism and Japanese imperialism? It's an unpleasant fact, but sometimes you need to make war to bring peace. As George Orwell explained, "People sleep peaceably in their beds at night only because rough men stand ready to do violence on their behalf."

In fact, if it hadn't been for the force of arms, America wouldn't even exist. We established the U.S. as an independent country only after winning the American Revolution against the British. Should we try to make amends by giving the country back to the Queen? We also took Texas and much of the Western United States from Mexico and Spain. Should we now send Jimmy Carter to Mexico to give back this land like he gave back the Panama Canal? Remember, the world has been a very bloody place for a long, long time. Most people today occupy land that was conquered and taken from somebody else.

And of course, we fought the Indians as well, a fact that liberals decry as a kind of American original sin. What they don't mention is that long before Columbus sailed the ocean blue in 1492, North American Indians were fighting, torturing, and raping one another—and (listen up, you nanny state-loving liberals) even smoking. Contrary to today's fashionable myth that Indians were gentle pacifists, they inflicted plenty of damage on settlers and on each other. Many settlers were killed during Indian raids. (For you Hollywood liberal types, think Daniel Day-Lewis in *Last of the Mohicans*.)

Conquest is a constant of human history. Today, radical Muslims around the world have declared their intention to transform the world into a unified Islamic state. Would

War: What is it good for?

- Overthrowing a genocidal dictator (Iraq War)
- Overthrowing an Islamic fundamentalist regime that harbored the architects of the September 11 attacks (Invasion of Afghanistan)
- Ending Saddam Hussein's rape of Kuwait (Gulf War)
- Kicking a communist army out of South Korea (Korean War)
- Freeing Europe from Nazi tyranny (World War II)
- Freeing Asia from marauding Japanese troops (World War II)
- Stopping German submarines from sinking U.S. merchant ships (World War I)
- Ending slavery in America and preserving the union (Civil War)
- Ending the impressment of U.S. sailors into the British Navy (War of 1812)
- Securing American independence from the British (War of Independence)

Osama bin Laden take our country from us if he could? You bet. Thus, even today we possess our country not because we have title insurance or a deed registered in some courthouse—we defend it by force of arms. Every day the U.S. depends on its military to stop others from taking our country. If you can't defend your land by force, then you probably won't own it for long.

LIBERAL LUNACY:
"No blood for oil!"

In reality, the Iraq invasion had little to do with oil. If the U.S. simply wanted to use war to get free or cheaper oil, we could have kept Kuwait's oil fields for ourselves back in 1991. Heck, in 1991 the U.S. could have moved its 550,000 troops on the ground into Iraq itself to capture the oil fields; after all, Iraq had no army left to oppose us. Who could have stopped us? Why have we been paying market prices for Kuwaiti and Iraqi oil ever since?

If America wanted to use its military might just to conquer or to steal oil, then why didn't we move southward and seize the Mexican or Venezuelan oil fields? It would have been a whole lot cheaper to take oil fields south of the border than to send our carrier groups halfway around the world. Besides, if all we wanted was cheaper oil, the U.S. would've simply given in to French and German demands to lift the economic sanctions on Iraq in the 1990s.

Just because the Iraq War is not about oil, however, does not mean that we should never fight for oil. Author Ann Coulter said it best: "Why not go to war for oil? We need oil." How else do we expect to keep the lights, refrigerators, and cars running? Don't we want our homes heated in the winter and cooled in the summer?

LIBERAL LUNACY:
"George Bush lied about WMD and the dangers posed by Saddam."

So, President Bush conspired with British prime minister Tony Blair, Secretary of State Colin Powell, Secretary of

Defense Donald Rumsfeld, and the American and British military and intelligence services to fabricate reasons for invading Iraq? If President Bush were really that sinister, wouldn't he have been deceptive enough to have actually planted some WMD? How hard would it have been to have someone drop a vial of anthrax in a Baghdad basement? In fact, Saddam's lack of cooperation with international inspectors left the world with no choice but to assume he had WMDs.

Remember, the U.S.-led coalition stopped fighting the 1991 Persian Gulf War only because Saddam agreed not only to give up his WMD programs, but also to bear the burden of proving that he did so. Yet, Saddam never came close to satisfying this burden, for he repeatedly lied for a decade about his internal weapons development and even kicked out UN weapons inspectors from Iraq in 1998. We know that Saddam developed and used WMD because he used them against both the Iranians and the Kurds.

According to the Interim Progress Report delivered to Congress in October 2003, investigators in Iraq located dozens of WMD-related program activities and large amounts of equipment that Iraq concealed from UN weapons inspectors, as well as strains of biological organisms that could be used to make biological weapons (concealed in a scientist's home).

We also learned from David Kay, former head of the Iraqi Survey Group, that the evidence of Saddam's intent to acquire WMD is undisputed. In his January 2004 testimony before the U.S. Senate, Kay explained that Saddam, in violation of UN resolutions, had a missile program that had the potential to incorporate WMD in their warheads.

According to Kay, UN inspectors had found enormous quantities of banned chemical and biological weapons in Iraq in the 1990s and Saddam "certainly could have produced small amounts" of chemical and biological weapons. He even went so far as to conclude that Iraq "was in the early stages of renovating [its nuclear weapon program]." He also noted "There's absolutely no doubt" that, if still in power, Saddam would harbor ambitions to develop and use WMD. Kay agreed that toppling Saddam was wholly justified and, in doing so, the security of the United States and the world was enhanced.

Saddam was clearly a threat, and the fact that some of our intelligence on Saddam's WMD program turned out to be incorrect doesn't make the war unjust.

And let's not forget who was responsible for configuring the intelligence community at the time. Bill Clinton's policies decimated American intelligence during the 1990s, so if anyone is to blame for poor intelligence, it'd be Clinton.

That's right: blame Clinton. In 2002, then CIA director George Tenet, a leftover from the Clinton administration, was asked by President Bush point-blank about Saddam's WMD. Tenet declared, "It's a slam dunk." Now, let's think about this for a second. If you are the president of the United States and your CIA director tells you that Saddam possessing WMD is a "slam-dunk" case, then how can you not believe him? How can anyone know more about foreign intelligence than the director of the Central Intelligence Agency? No one can. So, when Clinton appointee George Tenet told President Bush that Saddam had WMD, what was the president supposed to do? Keep in mind how the Left screamed that Bush failed to diligently protect the country from terrorism by not acting on a nondescript general memo, prepared before September 11, about Osama bin Laden wanting to destroy America.

If, according to the Left, Bush should have acted forcefully on that memo, then what would have happened if Bush had ignored Tenet's "slam dunk" declaration and an Iraqi WMD later hit Chicago? How could Bush have justified not acting on clear CIA intelligence? He couldn't have, and the Left would have attacked him viciously.

In 1998 a far-sighted politician said:

❝ We gave Saddam a chance, not a license. If we turn our backs on his defiance, the credibility of U.S. power as a check against Saddam will be destroyed. We will not only have allowed Saddam to shatter the inspection system that controls his weapons of mass destruction; we will also have fatally undercut the fear of force that stops Saddam from acting to gain domination of the region. ❞ [8]

Who said it? Bill Clinton.

VRWC TALKING POINTS

★ For jihadists, our presence in Iraq is just one of many grievances. If we withdraw, we'll embolden the terrorists and give them the opportunity to attack us elsewhere—like in an American city.

★ There's nothing about Iraq's "civil war" that makes our mission there unwinnable. To the contrary, it's better to fight a divided enemy than a united one.

★ We are suffering nowhere near the scale of casualties in Iraq that we suffered during the Vietnam War.

* Wars aren't fought according to timetables. Setting a timetable for withdrawal from Iraq would just demonstrate a lack of conviction in our mission there.

* We don't need the approval of corrupt, despotic, and unfriendly governments in the UN to pursue our national interests in Iraq or anywhere else.

* Opposing the Iraq mission is no more "moral" than supporting it, whether or not one has served in the military.

* The money spent in Iraq is a pittance compared to the cost of allowing another terrorist attack on U.S. soil.

* Displaying peace signs and singing "Give Peace a Chance" are touchy-feely, "feel good" efforts that accomplish little more than higher sales for bumper sticker companies. Wars are sometimes necessary to protect human life and freedom.

* If the U.S. were involved in the Middle East only for oil, we never would have given up control of Kuwait's oil fields.

* President Bush didn't lie about Saddam's WMD programs. He received faulty intelligence from a Clinton-appointee at the CIA. Regardless, Saddam had used WMDs before and looked set to use them again.

SOCIAL SECURITY AND OTHER ENTITLEMENTS: OUR FAILED EXPERIMENT IN SOCIALISM

The government wants to take care of the elderly through Social Security. It wants to attend to the sick through Medicare and Medicaid. It wants to protect the unemployed through welfare. What do all these programs have in common? They don't work.

* * * * *

LIBERAL LUNACY:
"The talk about the Social Security system being broken is just a bunch of hype."

Social Security is run by the federal government—there's the first problem right there. The government was not designed to be a mutual fund, a savings and loan, or a national pension scheme. Using the government for these purposes is like going to a homeless shelter for a place to stay—you'll get the basic minimum, but in the long run you'll want something better.

The Social Security system is in big trouble. According to the Social Security Trustees report, Social Security will start paying out more in benefits than it collects in taxes as early as 2018.[1] The Social Security trust fund will likely remain solvent for a few decades after that by collecting interest and some other income, but the trust fund surplus is expected to be depleted in 2042 according to the Social Security Administration, or in 2052 according to the Congressional Budget Office. As Fed Chairman Ben Bernanke commented, "the imperative to undertake reform earlier rather than later is great."[2]

Social Security is a pay-as-you-go system. This means that taxes taken out of your paycheck today go directly to pay the benefits of current retirees. Any money left over is not invested in the system, but is diverted to other government spending programs. The Social Security trust fund that Al Gore famously promised to lock up in an iron-clad cage perched on a mountaintop and protected by an environmentally friendly fire-breathing dragon is really an illusion. The fund does not contain any assets other than U.S. government bonds that function as IOUs between different parts of the government.

In 2018, when the system begins paying out more than it receives, the only way to keep the system solvent will be to redeem the bonds in the trust fund. But in order to do that, we'll either have to raise taxes, cut spending, or reduce benefits. Make no mistake about it—Social Security is heading toward insolvency.

For those liberals who are willing to face reality and admit there's a problem, the main solution they propose is—surprise, surprise—higher taxes! Barack Obama for example, has suggested that a massive tax hike "on the rich" could shore up the entire social security system.[3] Other liberal suggestions include boosting the retirement age, cutting benefits, or simply doing nothing at all.[4]

LIBERAL LUNACY:

"The current Social Security system is a good, 'guaranteed' investment."

Social Security is a terrible investment, offering a lower rate of return than just about any conventional investment vehicle. A twenty-five-year-old man will likely receive a -0.82 percent rate of return on his Social Security taxes. The rate is even lower for African Americans and other groups with shorter average life spans.[6] Moreover, your Social Security payments can't be passed on to your family after you die. No matter how much you've paid into the system, your return is flushed down the big government commode once you're no longer around to collect.

> **Enjoy It While It's Free**
>
> 66 Senator Obama would probably tax the air we breathe if that were possible. 99
>
> —Republican National Committee spokesman Brian Walton, on Barack Obama's proposal for a huge tax increase to fund Social Security.[5]

And what kind of "guarantee" is there that you'll receive even this measly payout after you retire? None! Your Social Security, in fact, is not guaranteed at all. In the 1960 case *Fleming v. Nestor*, the Supreme Court ruled that the money you spend your life paying into the Social Security system is controlled by Congress. You, the payer, have no legal rights to it whatsoever. This means that Congress can cut or even eliminate your benefits whenever it wants. Of course, if you trust politicians to always keep their promises, then you have nothing to worry about. And I'm sure senators like John "I voted for the war before I voted against it" Kerry and Jon "I was against amnesty before I was for it" Kyl are absolutely trustworthy when they promise that Social Security will always be there for us.

LIBERAL LUNACY:
"Adding private accounts to the Social Security system would be an expensive, risky gamble."

Conservatives propose a market-based solution to saving Social Security. Sometimes called "partial-privatization," these plans would allow workers to put a small percentage of their Social Security taxes into personal retirement accounts invested in a conservative mix of stock and bond funds.

The program would be purely voluntary, allowing any workers to remain totally invested in the current Social Security system. But it's unlikely that many would elect to do so, since the entire history of the stock and bond markets indicates that the long-term return even on conservative investments would far exceed the near-zero rate of return of the Social Security system.

When President Bush campaigned for Social Security reform in 2005, Democrats demagogued the issue to senior citizens, warning that their benefits would be eliminated in favor of risky private accounts. This couldn't be further from the truth. According to partial privatization plans, current seniors, in fact, would not even be eligible for private accounts, which would kick-in voluntarily among younger workers. Current Social Security beneficiaries would continue to collect their full benefits, just as before.

But liberals don't like privatizing anything. They view the government's rightful job as taking from the "rich" and giving to the "poor." Do you really want your retirement controlled by a government that acts like some incompetent Robin Hood? Hillary Clinton, Barack Obama, and John Edwards should wear green tights when they talk about "shoring up" the current Social Security system. Private accounts have met with success elsewhere. In Chile, for example, the return on workers' private retirement accounts has been 10 percent above inflation—an astounding improvement over the U.S. system.[7] Even contributing just 4 percentage points of payroll taxes, which is a level commonly discussed in Social Security reform plans, into a private account would add hundreds of thousands of dollars to the average retirees' lifetime benefits.

The odds of losing your shirt in the private accounts are pretty slim, since the choices would be limited to conservative, stable investments. But even if some investor with the luck and timing of original Beatles' drummer Pete Best lost everything, he'd still have the vast majority of his regular Social Security benefits to fall back on. What's more, the private accounts would be controlled by you, not the government. When you die, you could pass it on to your kids, your friends, or even Leona Helmsley's dog. Who knows? Who cares? It'd be your money and you could do whatever you want with it.

Stop the Presses: the *Washington Post* Supports a Bush Proposal

" Mr. Bush's sympathizers are right that Social Security privatization could reduce long-term deficits and right that the nation should not be deterred by the transition costs."

—*Washington Post*[8]

LIBERAL LUNACY:
"Medicare and Medicaid are vital,
efficient government programs."

Socialized medicine is a popular liberal cause. In her latest attempt to resurrect her failed health care reform of 1993, Hillary Clinton proposed *requiring* every American to buy health insurance. That's right, whether you want it or not, you're going to buy it, because that's what Nanny in Chief Hillary wants. Hillary has not yet explained the punishment that will be meted out to those that defy her wishes. Will she imprison those who don't buy health insurance? Fine them? Prevent them from getting a job? As Mark Steyn noted about Hillary's plan, "It's perfectly fine to employ legions of the undocumented from Mexico, but if you employ a fit twenty-six-year-old American with no health insurance either you or he or both of you will be breaking the law."[9]

Liberal luminaries like Hillary Clinton and Michael Moore insist that health care represents some kind of tragic market failure that can only be remedied by the great God of government control. To listen to them, you'd think that U.S. cities are teeming with old, poor, uninsured people dying on street corners because they can't afford health insurance.

Well, here's a newsflash: we already have a socialized health care system. It's run through Medicare and Medicaid. As of 2003, nearly half (44 percent) of all medical care consumed in the United States is financed by the government, largely through those two programs.[10]

What's more, like nearly all massive government programs, both these schemes are incredibly inefficient. This is because in both programs, prices are not set by market forces. Instead, bureaucrats arbitrarily set prices, creating all kinds of market distortions. Can some pencil pusher in Washington, D.C., really pinpoint the "correct" price of a certain medical procedure better than the market can, which subtly accounts for the galaxy of costs and demands inherent in every transaction? As John Lott observed, "Analysts and politicians can study trends for years without being able to account for all the factors that go into a single price."[11]

As a result of these misguided attempts at central price planning, the Cato Institute has found that Medicare and Medicaid are characterized by "increased demand, overconsumption, higher prices, and enormous waste." A study by Dartmouth academics found that nearly 20 percent of Medicare spending is wasted, a figure that translated to over $58 billion in 2005.[12]

Unsurprisingly, as spending on federal programs tends to do, spending on Medicare and Medicaid has increased astronomically. In fact, Medicare spending hit $408 billion in 2006, making it the largest federal program after the Department of Defense.[13] The Office of Management and Budget predicted Medicare and Medicaid will occupy an astounding one-fourth of federal outlays by 2009. The programs will only remain solvent through giant tax increases.[14]

The government's reaction to this crisis was predictable—instead of reducing the programs in favor of private competition, in 2003 it approved a new, outrageously expensive Medicare prescription drug benefit. This cost an estimated $26 billion in 2006 alone, and the price tag is projected to rise rapidly in the coming years.[15]

Nothing to Fear Here— Just National Bankruptcy

❝ Without change, rising costs [for Social Security and Medicare] will drive government spending to unprecedented levels, consume nearly all projected federal revenues and threaten America's future prosperity. ❞

—Henry M. Paulson Jr., secretary of the Treasury and a trustee of the Social Security and Medicare trust funds[16]

With the greatest and most innovative private health system in the world, why are we shoveling ever more money into the less efficient government health sector? The Medicare and Medicaid programs need to be radically curtailed in favor of a competitive private system. The government's health care Politburo, with its central planning of prices, is distorting the free market. Let doctors and insurance companies freely compete without government interference and the consumer will reap healthy benefits.

LIBERAL LUNACY:
"We need government welfare to redistribute wealth."

I don't know what causes it. Maybe they failed to advance beyond their freshman course in Marxism. But for whatever reason, liberals endlessly moan about how the rich get richer and the poor get poorer, and that it's not fair that some people can fly first class while others supposedly can't afford bicycles. Their solution is for the government to take money from the rich, use it to create social programs, and then spend the money on the poor, wasting much of it in the process.

Liberals fail to acknowledge a wise old adage: if you give someone a fish, you feed them for a day; but if you teach someone to fish, they feed themselves for a lifetime. The government should encourage the poor to acquire the skills and knowledge to become rich, not toss them handouts that create debilitating government dependency. Undoubtedly, some liberals really want to help the poor. But their policies are counterproductive, because they prioritize feelings over results. They don't respect poor people—they pity them. They want to show their compassion simply by giving money or other benefits to those in need. Liberals care about the symbolism of their policies more than the outcomes. They know that welfare robs people of initiative and breeds dependence, but that's doesn't matter to them. What's important is that they can point to their support for these programs as evidence of their how much they "care."

The Left has been trotting out the same old class warfare rhetoric for over a century. Why is it unfair for a rich person to make lots of money? Imagine if a young woman, Noelle, gets rich after working forty hours a week to pay for college—and studying another forty hours each week. Now imagine if this young lady had gone to high school with Jack, a guy who decided not to go to college or to get a decent job, and who never did anything to develop any marketable skills. Ten years later, Jack is lucky to find work sweeping up at McDonald's. Noelle has a Park Avenue penthouse. Is that unfair? Not on your life. Noelle's own work and self-sacrifice made her wealthy.

But how would a liberal view this little scenario? A liberal would immediately label Noelle a member of the "fortunate few," and conclude that she should be punished for her high income by being made to pay high taxes for social welfare programs—which go to benefit poor old Jack. At the ballot box, liberals can count on Jack for political support because, obviously, Jack is happy to get a piece of Noelle's income. Conservatives look at this same situation and understand that Noelle gets paid more not because she is lucky or because the system doesn't work, but because it does: Her skills and personal qualities (determination, perseverance) paid off in the marketplace. Nothing unfair about that.

Furthermore, welfare hurts the exact people it is meant to help. By paying people to remain unemployed and giving extra subsidies to non-working parents who had additional children, between the 1960s and the 1990s welfare policies perpetuated poverty by removing the incentive to work while adding to exploding rates of illegitimacy. Since Congress approved comprehensive welfare reform in 1996, however, we've seen dramatic improvements in child poverty and illegitimacy rates.[17] What a surprise—when the government stops paying people to be unemployed and to have kids out of wedlock, people find more jobs and have less out-of-wedlock children. Who could have predicted that?

LIBERAL LUNACY:
"Without welfare, life below the poverty line would be intolerable."

Come on. This is America—not Bangladesh! As economist Stephen Moore remarked, "Most Americans who are considered 'poor' today have routine access to a quality of housing, food, health care, consumer products, entertainment, communications, and transportation that even the

The Jury Is In: Less Welfare = Less Poverty[18]

- Since the 1996 welfare reform, welfare caseloads have declined by 56 percent.

- During the late 1990s, employment of never-married mothers grew by nearly 50 percent, of single mothers who are high school dropouts by 66 percent, and of young single mothers by nearly 100 percent.

- The child poverty rate fell from 20.8 percent in 1995 to 17.8 percent in 2004.

- Six years after welfare was reformed, the poverty rates for black children and for children from single-mother families fell to their lowest rates in history.

Vanderbilts, the Carnegies, the Rockefellers, and the nineteenth-century European princes, with all their wealth, could not have afforded."[19]

Robert Rector of the Heritage Foundation clarifies our terms: "For most Americans, the word 'poverty' suggests destitution: an inability to provide a family with nutritious food, clothing, and reasonable shelter. But only a small number of the 37 million persons classified as 'poor' by the Census Bureau fit that description. While real material hardship certainly does occur, it is limited in scope and severity. Most of America's 'poor' live in material conditions that would be judged as comfortable or well-off just a few generations ago."[20] Statistics back this up: 43 percent of "poor" households own their own homes, 80 percent have air conditioning, almost three-quarters own a car, 97 percent have a color TV, and 62 percent have cable or satellite TV. Not exactly the poverty Americans experienced in covered wagons.[21]

Pointing out such statistics will inevitably spark accusations from liberals that we conservatives are "uncompassionate." Well, let me tell you something. Conservatives are far more compassionate—and a whole lot less patronizing—than liberals. Liberals think it's "compassionate" to raise taxes on hardworking, productive Americans in order to transfer other people's money to Democratic constituents: welfare recipients and government bureaucrats.

In stark contrast, conservatives show real compassion by trying to create an equal playing field with as many economic opportunities as possible for everyone. Encouraging poor workers to find jobs and become self-reliant is far more compassionate than encouraging dependence on government handouts. Conservatives are vilified for being "mean," but that's an unjustified smear. We just care about results. We know that subsidizing undesirable behavior encourages more of that behavior. If you pay Bob to sit on his butt and eat Cheetos all day, he's probably going to keep doing it. Heck, if you paid me enough money, that's all I'd do, too. Most people aren't going to work if they don't have to. That's why it's called "work." But what happens when we cruel conservatives cut off Bob's welfare checks? Bob's forced to get a job. He's forced to become a responsible member of society. In short, he's forced to reclaim his dignity by earning his own living.

And so I ask my liberal friends: What's so mean about that?

VRWC TALKING POINTS

★ Social Security is headed toward bankruptcy and requires comprehensive reform.

★ For the young, Social Security offers a near-zero rate of return. Contrary to popular belief, there is no "guarantee" at all that you will receive even these meager payouts.

★ Adding private accounts to the Social Security system is a modest, voluntary reform that would lead to much higher returns on your investment.

★ Medicare and Medicaid are hugely expensive and grossly inefficient programs representing the partial socialization of our health care system.

★ Welfare punishes the rich for their success while hurting the poor it is meant to help.

★ Although real poverty exists in America, most of those defined as "poor" today enjoy relatively comfortable living conditions.

ABORTION:
WHY LIFE IS THE RIGHT CHOICE

Liberals will travel to the Arctic Circle on crusades to save baby seals. They'll launch pressure campaigns against tuna companies to protect baby dolphins from fishing nets. But when it comes to saving baby humans, they say "Hey, who are we to oppose a woman's *'choice?'*"

* * * * *

LIBERAL LUNACY:
"The abortion issue was settled by *Roe v. Wade.*"

Judging by the primary role the abortion issue plays in today's political debates, it clearly wasn't settled by one bad judicial decision in 1973. In fact, abortion doesn't belong in the courts at all—since there's no mention of the issue in the Constitution, its resolution is supposed to be left to the states.

The fact that a few judges have robbed the American people of a voice in such a vital matter is what keeps this such a divisive issue in American society. As President Reagan noted, "the Court's decision has by no means settled the debate. Instead, *Roe v. Wade* has become a continuing prod to the conscience of the nation."[1] *Roe v. Wade* is a textbook example of judicial overreach and should be overturned. The Supreme Court has reversed its own bad rulings before, and this should be no exception.

Contrary to the claims of many pro-abortion activists, overturning *Roe v. Wade* would not result in a nationwide ban on abortion. It would simply return the issue to the states, where the people, either through their legislative representatives or perhaps by referendum, could decide for themselves whether abortion would be legal or illegal.

The only means to protect the unborn nationwide is through a constitutional amendment banning abortion. But it will probably take many more years of grassroots work before there will be enough support for such a measure. Until then, the only constitutional option is to allow the people of each state to decide their own abortion policy. This is how our federal form of government is meant to work. Liberals, however, know that many states, if given a choice, would vote against legalized abortion. So they depend on the Supreme Court to act as a super legislature and force a pro-abortion policy on the entire population.

Letting the people decide through constitutional means may be a novel, even scary, concept to activist judges and pro-abortion partisans, but the Constitution's framers held the concept in pretty high regard. And so should we.

LIBERAL LUNACY:
"Banning abortion will force women to resort to back-alley abortions."

Women will not be "forced" into anything. Women are autonomous human beings who make decisions and face the consequences of their own actions, for better or worse. No one will be "forced" into an illegal abortion. Any illegal abortion will be a deliberate choice.

As we all know, there is one guaranteed way to avoid having an unwanted child—don't have sex. Feminists ridicule the very concept of chastity, which seems to be the only sexual "choice" they don't support. Instead, they advocate birth control because contraception, unlike chastity, requires no sexual self-restraint. Feminists view sex primarily as a recreational activity and a way to achieve personal fulfillment. What they refuse to acknowledge is that sex doesn't exist in nature to fill the emptiness in the lives of feminists. Sex exists for procreation. That's just Biology 101. This fact is not negated by birth control, which is never 100 percent effective anyway. Research by the pro-abortion Guttmacher Institute shows that 54 percent of women who have abortions use contraceptives in the month they get pregnant.[2] As they say in *Jurassic Park*, "Life finds a way." Pregnancy is the logical, natural outcome of a woman's choice to have sex.

Of course, a woman who has an unexpected pregnancy can always choose adoption over abortion. A woman "forced" into having an illegal abortion would thus have to reject chastity, refuse to raise the child, and reject adoption. As opposed to being "forced" into anything, she will have made repeated conscious choices that brought her to such dire straights. The notion that some greater cosmic power "forced" her into choosing an abortion is simply not true. And the innocent life she carries inside her should not be made to suffer the fatal consequences of her own choices.

LIBERAL LUNACY:
"Pro-abortion activists are caring 'moderates,' whereas pro-life activists are intolerant 'extremists.'"

Moderates, eh? Is that why the pro-abortion movement fought tooth and nail to keep partial-birth abortion legal?

According to the American Medical Association, partial birth abortion (which the AMA calls "intact dilation and extraction," or "D&X") is a procedure consisting of the following: "deliberate dilatation of the cervix, usually over a sequence of days; instrumental or manual conversion of the fetus to a footling breech; breech extraction of the body excepting the head; and partial evacuation of the intracranial contents of the fetus to effect vaginal delivery of a dead but otherwise intact fetus."[3]

In layman's terms, this describes the practice of partly delivering a baby, vacuuming his brains out, crushing his skull, and then delivering the rest of the now-dead baby. For years, pro-abortion activists insisted this barbaric practice was an extremely rare procedure occasionally required when the health of the mother was at risk. With these arguments, they convinced judges to overturn a variety of state and federal laws banning the procedure.

These arguments, however, turned out to be false. Planned Parenthood for several years argued that there were about 650—or at most under a thousand—partial birth abortions performed every year. These claims were debunked when a New Jersey reporter revealed that a single clinic was performing 1,500 partial-birth abortions annually. Shortly thereafter, Ron Fitzsimmons, executive director of the National Coalition of Abortion Providers, estimated that between 3,000 and 5,000 such procedures were performed every year.[4]

As for the necessity of partial-birth abortion, the American Medical Association declared that partial-birth abortion is never medically necessary, while the American College of Obstetricians and Gynecologists insists that there are no circumstances in which partial-birth abortion would be the only procedure that could save a woman's life or health.[5] Congress repeatedly voted to ban the procedure in the 1990s, but President Clinton vetoed these efforts. Congress again outlawed partial-birth abortion in 2003 and, after several courts overturned the ban, it was eventually upheld in 2007 by a one-person majority on the Supreme Court.

Why would "moderate" pro-abortion organizations deceive the public about this horrific form of infanticide in hopes of preserving its legality? Because they are ideologically vested in perpetuating all forms of abortion. The pro-life activists, on the other hand, simply fought to keep babies from having their brains sucked out. I ask you: Who holds the "extreme" position on this issue?

Fear and Loathing, NOW-style

" NOW [The National Organization for Women] would 'test' messages to see which would bring in the most dollars. Abortion rights and all its 'sky is falling' rhetoric frightened people the most and hence were the biggest moneymakers. The more you could make your membership base feel as though the end of the world were approaching and women would be thrown back into the kitchen, barefoot, pregnant, and lobotomized, the more the money poured in. It didn't matter if the message was accurate or fair, or even realistic. If it made money, it would run. "

—Tammy Bruce, former president of the Los Angeles chapter of the National Organization for Women, on NOW's manipulation of the abortion issue.[6]

LIBERAL LUNACY:
"It's hypocritical to oppose abortion while supporting capital punishment."

Not every pro-life advocate supports the death penalty. But some do, and there's no inconsistency in holding these two positions. In opposing abortion, pro-lifers oppose the killing of an absolutely innocent life. An unborn baby has hurt no one, has done no wrong, and does not deserve to be snuffed out simply because his birth would be inconvenient to the parents.

This is certainly not the case for those sentenced to capital punishment. Here, we're dealing with the worst murderers and other violent criminals that one can imagine. The difference between an unborn baby and a death row inmate is that the criminal is not *innocent*. He has committed one or more heinous crimes and is now facing the consequences of his own actions.

In our judicial system, we punish the guilty, not the innocent. Supporting the death penalty while opposing abortion is perfectly consistent with this tradition.

LIBERAL LUNACY:
"Abortion reduces crime."

This theory was popularized by the best-selling book *Freakonomics*, in which the authors, Steven Levitt and Stephen Dubner, argue that the large number of babies aborted after the *Roe v. Wade* decision in 1973 would likely have been "unwanted" kids born to poor or teenage mothers, and would have been highly likely to turn into criminals. But because they were aborted, they did not to grow up to commit the crimes expected of them, thus leading to a remarkable drop in crime rates in the 1990s.

The theory is fairly repugnent, as it runs perilously close to an argument for racial eugenics. As Levitt and Dubner likely know, yet for some reason chose not to mention in their book, abortions in America are disproportionately performed on black babies.[7]

What's more, economists have now shown that the argument has empirical mistakes as well. Not only did the authors run flawed statistical tests,[8] but other studies show that legalized abortion actually *increases* crime by increasing the rates of premarital sex and out-of-wedlock births. A study by economists John Whitley and John Lott found that legalizing abortion increased the murder rate by an average of 7 percent.[9]

So, Levitt and Dubner leave us with a wonderful theory! If we were just to abort every baby in America, crime would eventually fall to zero! Sorry guys, but back to the drawing board. If you want to fight crime, it's better to hire more cops than to abort more babies.

LIBERAL LUNACY:
"We're not pro-abortion, we're pro-choice."

This is a clever rhetorical dodge and nothing more. In practice, if you're not expressly against abortion, you are at least implicitly in favor of it. What if a group appeared in America tomorrow advocating the legalization of slavery, explaining, "We're not in favor of slavery. We just want the right to choose whether to own a slave." Everyone would recognize that this group was really pro-slavery. Any attempt to portray the "pro-choice" position as abortion-neutral is

just as ridiculous. Pro-abortion groups can hardly be described as observers standing on the abortion sidelines.

Saying that one is in favor of the "choice" to abort assumes that abortion is a valid moral choice, just as being
pro-choice on slavery necessarily assumes that slavery is
not immoral.

LIBERAL LUNACY:
"The fetus is not a human being."

"Life begins," said former Democratic presidential candidate Wesley Clark a few years ago, "with the mother's decision." So I guess infanticide is just fine if that's what Mom
wants? Let's bring on those seventh-trimester abortions!

In reality, a "human being" is a living member of the
species *Homo sapiens*. Leaving aside the self-serving political
posturing, objective science can determine without a reasonable doubt whether any living thing is a human being.
A human being, from the moment of fertilization, is ge-
netically complete. To quote professor Jerome Lejeune: "If
a fertilized egg is not by itself a full human being, it could
never become a man, because something would have to
be added to it, and we know that does not happen."

When does human life begin? Biologically, this isn't a
tough question. Regardless of whether one ultimately
supports legalized abortion, it is a scientific fact that human life begins at conception when a male sperm fertilizes
a female egg. Once joined, the sperm and egg form a new
individual human possessing its own unique genetic code.
About twenty-one days later, that "thing" in the womb
called a fetus has a heartbeat. The chromosomal composition of the newly formed individual remains unchanged
whether it is permitted to reach maturity in the form of

an infant at nine months or is terminated prematurely at six weeks. And, of course, if not aborted, the zygote inevitably grows into a human baby—not a frog, a cow, or a chicken.

What's the difference between a seven-day-old fetus and an eight-and-a-half-month-old fetus? If an eight-and-a-half-month-old fetus is a human entitled to legal protection, then why isn't a seven-day-old fetus entitled to the same protection? They both have the same unique genetic composition.

Humanity is not something one acquires, like a skill; you're either human or you're not. People may undergo socialization, societies may undergo civilization, but a human being cannot undergo humanization.

> ## CONSERVATIVES SAY IT BEST
>
> " I have often said that when we talk about abortion, we are talking about two lives— the life of the mother and the life of the unborn child. Why else do we call a pregnant woman a mother? I have also said that anyone who doesn't feel sure whether we are talking about a second human life should clearly give life the benefit of the doubt. If you don't know whether a body is alive or dead, you would never bury it. I think this consideration itself should be enough for all of us to insist on protecting the unborn. "
>
> —Ronald Reagan[10]

LIBERAL LUNACY:
"The decision to have an abortion is a woman's personal choice and the government should stay out of it."

This begs the ultimate question of whether the fetus is a human life. If a fetus is human, nobody has a right to kill it. This argument is like saying that you should have the personal choice to commit murder or rape and the government shouldn't interfere.

LIBERAL LUNACY:
"We should strive to make abortion 'safe, legal, and rare!' "

That's Bill Clinton's phrase: "safe, legal, and rare."[11] He succeeded in keeping abortions "legal," but they're neither safe nor rare. Abortions are never safe for the child being aborted, and they're often not safe for the mother, who can suffer from complications ranging from infertility to psychological trauma to death.

Rare? Not quite. Today, over 1 million abortions occur each year in the U.S. and over 42 million were performed between 1973, when abortion was legalized, and 2002.[12] But why does Clinton (or any other liberal) want to make abortions "rare," if aborting a fetus has the same moral significance as cutting your toenails?

LIBERAL LUNACY:
"Anti-abortion crusaders are motivated by religion, and they should not try to impose their religious views on others."

So the liberals want to eliminate religion from politics. Well, let's kiss goodbye those laws against murder and theft; after all, we derived them from the Ten Commandments. I guess we'll have to bring back slavery, too; the movement to outlaw it was driven largely by Northeastern abolitionists inspired by Judeo-Christian ethics.

Anyway, there is no religious creed that states: "The life of a human being starts at fertilization, when the father's sperm unites with the mother's egg." You will not find this sentiment in the Bible. The reason is simple. This is not a matter of faith, but of scientific fact. To call the results of this research "religious belief" is to call biology a religion.[13]

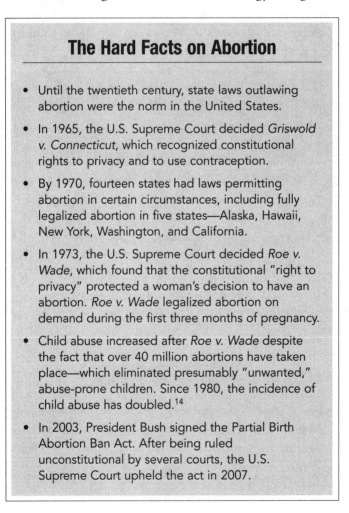

The Hard Facts on Abortion

- Until the twentieth century, state laws outlawing abortion were the norm in the United States.

- In 1965, the U.S. Supreme Court decided *Griswold v. Connecticut*, which recognized constitutional rights to privacy and to use contraception.

- By 1970, fourteen states had laws permitting abortion in certain circumstances, including fully legalized abortion in five states—Alaska, Hawaii, New York, Washington, and California.

- In 1973, the U.S. Supreme Court decided *Roe v. Wade*, which found that the constitutional "right to privacy" protected a woman's decision to have an abortion. *Roe v. Wade* legalized abortion on demand during the first three months of pregnancy.

- Child abuse increased after *Roe v. Wade* despite the fact that over 40 million abortions have taken place—which eliminated presumably "unwanted," abuse-prone children. Since 1980, the incidence of child abuse has doubled.[14]

- In 2003, President Bush signed the Partial Birth Abortion Ban Act. After being ruled unconstitutional by several courts, the U.S. Supreme Court upheld the act in 2007.

LIBERAL LUNACY:
"Every child should be a planned and wanted child. No child should be born unwanted."

"Wantedness" is a subjective measure of another's feelings. If a child can't be allowed to live unless or until he is wanted, this makes human life not valuable in itself. No one's life has value unless others deem it valuable. Following this line of liberal logic, the homeless probably aren't "wanted," either. Should we do away with them, too?

Every baby should be wanted—simply because every baby is in fact a human being. If he isn't wanted, the problem lies with his parents or society at large, not with the innocent baby. Why should babies have to die because of the selfishness of others? Contrary to the old pro-abortion promise that legal abortion would lower the number of "unwanted" children and thus reduce child abuse, if anything, the opposite has occurred. Despite the fact that over 40 million presumably unwanted children have been killed by abortion since *Roe v. Wade*, since 1980 the incidence of child abuse has doubled.[15] Legalized abortion has resulted in the devaluing of human life such that the birth of a former fetus is viewed by many as the result of just another lifestyle choice, rather than a sacred event.

VRWC TALKING POINTS

★ *Roe v. Wade* was a poorly reasoned decision that improperly asserted judicial power over the abortion issue. Because the people's voice was replaced by the dictates of nine unelected judges, abortion has become one of the most divisive social issues in America today.

★ If abortion were banned, women would not be "forced" into back alley abortions. Such procedures would only stem from women making a series of free choices.

★ Pro-abortion activists' disingenuous attempts to keep partial-birth abortion legal show them to be the extremists, not the moderates, in the abortion debate.

★ Supporting capital punishment while opposing abortion demonstrates a commonsense concern for punishing the guilty and protecting the innocent.

★ Legalized abortion does nothing to decrease crime, and in fact may increase it.

★ To support the "right" to abortion is to support the act of abortion itself as a legitimate moral choice.

★ The belief that "life begins at conception" is not a philosophical theory—it's a scientific fact.

★ If an unborn baby is a human being, then the government has the right to protect that baby from harm.

★ Promises to make abortion "safe, legal, and rare" result in keeping abortion legal, but neither safe nor rare.

★ Judeo-Christian ethics is a well-founded source of moral principles.

★ A human being derives his dignity simply from being human, not from being "wanted" by others.

MEDIA BIAS: ALL THE NEWS THAT FITS THE SLANT

The mainstream media continues its assault on virtually every policy associated with conservatives or the Bush administration. Meanwhile, liberals declare war on FOX News, talk radio, and any other media outlet that allows conservatives a voice.

★ ★ ★ ★ ★

LIBERAL LUNACY:
"FOX News exerts an evil, all-powerful influence in the media."

If you really want to throw a group of liberals into a wild-eyed fit of sputtering rage, tell them you watch FOX News. Then sit back, have a good laugh, and watch the saliva fly.

Liberals hate FOX News with a passion they usually reserve for Dick Cheney, gun owners, and heterosexual marriage. Why? To hear them tell it, you would think FOX News is the only news channel in America—an evil, gluttonous monopoly that indoctrinates every American into a fascistic credo. When the Congressional Black Caucus scheduled a FOX News debate among the Democratic presidential candidates for September 2007, Hillary Clinton, John Edwards, and Barack Obama all refused to join, and the debate was cancelled. In contrast, there were no boycotts when Republicans subjected themselves to the indignity of an MSNBC debate hosted by former Jimmy Carter speechwriter Chris Matthews, who asked his typically hard-hitting questions, like whether the candidates want to change the Constitution to allow Arnold Schwarzenegger to run for president.

The rise of FOX News has certainly given some balance to the media's overwhelmingly liberal tilt. But the channel is far from the malevolent, unstoppable juggernaut that trembling liberals imagine. Despite its successes, FOX News is still not even available in all areas of the country. When compared to the number of viewers that the network news broadcasts reach every night, FOX's supposedly all-powerful influence pales in comparison. For example, on any given weeknight, FOX News may draw an audience of 2–3 million to *The O'Reilly Factor*, while an average broadcast of NBC's Nightly News draws 9–10 million.

What liberals really can't stand is not FOX News' reach or power, but the fact that the network gives Americans one place to go on their TV dial that doesn't always buy into liberal bias. Liberals miss the good old days before cable TV, when a handful of liberal broadcasters monopolized the TV news and could dish out the liberal spin without any available alternative. In 1968, Walter Cronkite had a huge influence in turning Americans against the Vietnam War when the anchorman denounced the "unwinnable" conflict on CBS News. Nowadays, if Katie Couric were to pronounce the Iraq War unwinnable, the only thing that would shock most viewers would be that she knew a word with so many syllables.

LIBERAL LUNACY:
"We need to bring back the Fairness Doctrine to allow liberals a chance to succeed on talk radio."

Of all the underhanded Democratic moves leading up to the 2008 election, the attempt to resurrect the "Fairness Doctrine" has to be one of the most sinister.

There's no doubt that conservatives dominate talk radio—that's because people listen to them. There is no liberal version of Rush Limbaugh because nobody wants to listen to liberals. Just look at the sorry saga of Air America. After launching in 2004 as a liberal counterpoint to conservative talk radio, the network lost a ton of money. People simply refused to listen to Air America despite (or perhaps, because of) the presence of liberal stalwarts like Al Franken. Finally, the network filed for bankruptcy in 2006. Today, after being bailed out by liberal New York City real estate investor Stephen Green, Air America continues to limp along like a lame horse waiting to be put out of its misery. As Brian Maloney commented after the buy-out, "Much of the media coverage examines how Air America can be 'restored' to its supposed former glory. One problem: when did it ever succeed in the first place?"[1]

GreenStone Media suffered a similar fate. Founded as a feminist radio network in 2006 by Gloria Steinem, Jane Fonda, and other aging man-haters, the network secured funding, equipment, sympathetic publicity, and everything else needed for a successful network—except for an audience that wanted to listen to whining feminists. Lacking that key element, the network shut down in 2007 amidst claims from angry female employees that the station's founders refused to provide any severance pay.[2]

Rejected by the American public, liberals turned to their perennial solution to every problem: government regulation. Liberal politicians decided that if liberal radio couldn't compete in the market, they'd legislate it into the market. In 2007, Democratic congressman Dennis Kucinich and Democratic senators Dick Durbin, Dianne Feinstein, and John Kerry all advocated a revival of the Fairness Doctrine, an FCC regulation that required broadcasters to air both sides of political issues. The FCC abolished the doctrine in 1987, but liberals want to bring it back in order to snuff out conservative radio. Under the Fairness Doctrine, stations that broadcast a conservative show would have to offset it by broadcasting a liberal show. Since no one listens to liberal shows, many stations would probably just abandon their conservative hosts rather than add in liberal shows that drive their ratings into the ground.

Liberals argue that the lack of leftwing radio shows stems from structural problems in radio regulations and a lack of diversity among station owners.[3] In other words, liberals aren't given a chance to succeed in talk radio. However, as the failure of Air America, GreenStone Media, and many other liberal talk show hosts demonstrates, this is totally untrue. In fact, new liberal networks can almost always depend on lots of sympathetic coverage from the mainstream media. For example, a Nexis search shows that the *New York Times* dedicated thirteen stories to Air America just in 2004, the year of its launch. The truth is, liberals have no problem getting into the market. It's just that once they're there, they can't compete. Their attempt to blame "the system" for the failures of their own talk show hosts is typical liberal tripe—it's always someone else's fault.

In contrast, the airwaves are full of successful conservatives, including Rush Limbaugh, Bill Bennett, G. Gordon Liddy, Michael Medved, Matt Drudge, Michael

Liberal Failure on the Airwaves

The long list of liberals who have started radio shows only to have them cancelled due to a lack of listener interest includes:

- actress Janeane Garofalo
- former New York governor Mario Cuomo
- former Texas agriculture commissioner Jim Hightower
- Harvard Law professor Alan Dershowitz
- former presidential candidate Gary Hart
- former Connecticut governor Lowell Weicker
- former New York Democratic mayor Ed Koch
- former California Democratic governor Jerry Brown
- former Virginia governor Douglas Wilder

Reagan, Michael Savage, Bill O'Reilly, Laura Ingraham, Sean Hannity, and Hugh Hewitt, to name just a few. Sidestepping the liberal stranglehold on the major media, these talented conservatives give people a consumer choice. And when the American people are given a choice, they choose conservative.

LIBERAL LUNACY:
"The *New York Times* has no liberal bias.
If anything, it leans conservative."

Can you believe that liberal media critic Eric Alterman actually makes this claim? I wonder what color the sky is in Altermanland.

Alterman asserts that the *Times'* political coverage "is actually driven by the Far Right's agenda," although he's willing to concede that the paper's editorial page leans liberal "of late."[4] And how late is that? Exactly how long has the *Times* editorial page been liberal? Here's a hint: the *Times* hasn't endorsed a Republican presidential candidate since Dwight Eisenhower.[5] That's right, the last time the *Times* recommended a Republican for president, news of the endorsement wasn't delivered to all fifty states—because we didn't have fifty states yet.

This really should come as no surprise from a paper that is so wedded to affirmative action that it continued to promote an obvious fraud, Jayson Blair, through the ranks of its newsroom despite abundant evidence that his articles were filled with mistakes and outright inventions. Blair, a national reporter for the *Times*, repeatedly wrote about places he'd never been, filed interviews with people he'd never met, and plagiarized from other newspapers. Yet the *Times* kept him employed for *four years*, allowing him to write over 600 articles.[6] In explaining the Blair fiasco, the *Times'* then executive editor, Howell Raines, reiterated the paper's "commitment to diversity," then added, "You have a right to ask if I, as a white man from Alabama, with those convictions, gave him one chance too many. . . . When I look into my heart for the truth of that, the answer is yes."[7]

Thus, since the *Times'* executive editor was a "white man from Alabama," the paper gave free reign to a journalistic fraud because the charlatan's skin color happened to be black. The prioritizing of "diversity" over competence dates back to 1994, when the paper's publisher, Arthur Sulzberger Jr. (then deputy publisher), declared that boosting the *Times'* racial, gender, and sexual-orientation diversity was "the single most important issue" confronting the paper.[8] Speaking about diversity-related issues in an interview that year, Sulzberger proclaimed that "increasingly, any middle or senior manager's or any employee's advancement is going to depend on how he or she deals with these fundamental issues."[9]

So the *Times* deems "diversity" so important that the paper will hinder the careers of employees who don't embrace it enthusiastically enough. Then it wonders how the fraud Jayson Blair got away with such blatant fabrications. One would think the *Times* would be more concerned with its plunging subscription numbers, or the fact that in October 2007 its stock price hit a ten-year low. Or perhaps the *Times* management would be investigating why, in September 2007, the paper had to cancel its online TimesSelect program, which forced readers to pay to see certain online content like the *Times'* columnists. (People seem to relate to Maureen Dowd columns like they do to a car wreck—they'll take a morbid look if it's there in front of them, but they're not going to go out of their way to see it). For the *Times* honchos, however, little things like plunging stock prices and failed business models are no reason for concern. "Diversity" is what counts.

With its omnipresent liberal slant, the *Times* is really just carrying on a grand tradition dating at least as far back as the 1930s. Then, Walter Duranty, the *Times* correspondent in Moscow, proudly regurgitated Stalin's propaganda about the glorious achievements of communism, going so far as to deny the existence of the Ukrainian famine that killed millions of people.

As for the Iraq War, the *Times* found that its constant antiwar drumbeat and unremitting focus on the worst news out of Iraq were simply not enough. It had to go one step further, revealing in 2005 the existence of the top secret Terrorist Surveillance Program that monitored the international communications of domestic terrorism suspects. Like a slobbering Pavlovian dog, the ACLU jumped on the case, filing a lawsuit that convinced a Jimmy Carter-appointed federal judge to rule the program illegal.

In July 2007 an appeals court overruled the judge, but the damage had already been done—thanks to the *Times*, terrorism suspects were tipped off that their calls and e-mails were being monitored, and phone companies stopped cooperating with the program for fear of lawsuits. In response, the government shut down the program and began petitioning the Foreign Intelligence Surveillance court (the FISA court) for warrants before wiretapping these kinds of communications. The *Times* could be proud that the government was again forced to fight terrorism as a purely police issue, having to show probable cause to a judge before being allowed to listen in on al Qaeda members discussing how to blow up American cities.

Unsurprisingly, as courts tend to do, the FISA court exceeded its authority and claimed jurisdiction over the monitoring of communications among foreign terrorism suspects if their communications were routed through American data networks. Even the Democrat-controlled Congress realized this went too far. In August 2007, Congress approved a bill temporarily allowing warrantless monitoring of these kinds of communications, as well as easing the restrictions on monitoring terrorism suspects

> ### New York Times to Osama bin Laden: "Our Weakness Is a Virtue."
>
> " The phone companies have limited their cooperation [with the Terrorist Surveillance Program] due to the risk of lawsuits following the *New York Times* exposure of the wiretap program in 2005. Mr. Bush's January decision to subject these wiretaps to the supervision of the special FISA court has eroded intelligence even further. In many cases, the National Security Agency now needs a warrant to tap even foreign-to-foreign contacts that happen to be routed through U.S. telephone switches. No wonder Osama bin Laden thinks America is a 'weak horse.' "
>
> —*Wall Street Journal*[10]

communicating between the U.S. and abroad. How did the *Times* react to this commonsense measure? It accused President Bush of "incessant fear-mongering" and instructed Democrats that their "most important duty" is to oppose Bush's national security agenda.[11] Did you get that? For the *Times*, opposing Bush is a higher priority than protecting Americans from terrorists.

With such a deep hostility to U.S. national security, it was no surprise when the *Times* violated its own policies by giving the radical antiwar group MoveOn.org a $77,508 discount on a full page advertisement. The ad was a scurrilous attack on the U.S. commander in Iraq, General Petraus, whom the ad charmingly referred to as "General Betray Us." After denying any wrongdoing for nearly two weeks, the *Times'* own public editor admitted that the ad should not have been discounted, nor should it have run at all, since it violated *Times* policies against printing ads that are personal attacks. A *Times* flak explained the episode simply as a "mistake."[12] It's funny how the *Times* never seems to mistakenly give conservative groups a $77,000 discount.

More recently, the *Times* again distinguished itself with its uncritical, cheerleading coverage of the prosecution of three innocent Duke lacrosse players for the falsely alleged rape of a Durham stripper. The *Times* thought it had a perfect case to fit its leftwing agenda—a group of supposedly rich, privileged white kids accused of gang raping a poor black woman. The paper leaped all over the case, abandoning any pretense of a presumption of innocence. "At the intersection of entitlement and enablement, there is Duke University, virtuous on the outside, debauched on the inside," exclaimed sports columnist Selena Roberts.[13] She then falsely asserted that lacrosse players had refused to cooperate with the police. The common thread between the Duke case and other instances where sports players refused to inform on their teammates, according to Selena, was the desire to "exploit the vulnerable without heeding a conscience."[14]

When a *Times* reporter submitted a story summarizing the defense lawyers' evidence that the players were innocent, the *Times* refused to the run the article. It quickly replaced the reporter with another one who was more sympathetic to the prosecution.[15] Nevertheless, the case soon unraveled after DNA testing turned up negative for all the lacrosse players. Other gaping holes appeared in the case, including constantly changing stories by the accuser and evidence that the police had rigged the photo lineup used to identify the suspects. The *Times* reacted to these developments by insisting that despite the obvious weaknesses in the case, "there is also a body of evidence to support [Durham DA Mike Nifong's] decision to take the matter to trial."[16]

DA Nifong was disbarred and even jailed over his handling of the case, and the North Carolina Attorney General dropped all charges after pronouncing the three Duke suspects innocent. This indicates there was never any body of evidence at all to prosecute the players. Following a public outcry over the *Times'* outrageous coverage of the attempt by a politically correct, rogue prosecutor to railroad three innocent kids, the *Times* public editor analyzed the paper's coverage of the case. He reached the predictable conclusion that "most flaws flowed from journalistic lapses rather than ideological bias."[17]

There's the *Times'* logo for you: We may be crummy journalists, but at least we're not biased.

LIBERAL LUNACY:
"The fact that mainstream newspapers supported the invasion of Iraq proves that they have no liberal bias."

True, the *Washington Post* endorsed the Iraq invasion. (The paper also used its endorsement as an opportunity to call on President Bush to scale back or drop his proposed tax cuts.)[18] But the *Post* has more than made up for its apostasy with its constant antiwar drumbeat, unremitting focus on the worst news out of Iraq, obsession with Abu Ghraib, and outright demonization of President Bush and Vice President Cheney.

As for the *New York Times,* while before the war it occasionally editorialized in favor of using force in Iraq, it was adamant that America could not wage war without the express approval of the United Nations. Just days before the attack on Iraq began, the *Times* denounced President Bush's war policy as "reckless."[18] And since the moment that war broke out, the *Times* has put the most negative spin possible on all our efforts in Iraq. When the U.S.-led coalition met with stunning success in its initial invasion of Iraq, what did the *Times* focus on? It printed around a dozen articles relating what turned out to be totally exaggerated allegations that the Iraq Museum had been looted.

The mainstream media has picked up where it left off after Vietnam. Determined to take down President Bush regardless of the cost to the country, the press deliberately skews its Iraq coverage to give the impression that there is no solution other than to give up and retreat. The reporting on Iraq is also affected by newspapers' heavy use of local Iraqi stringers to do the actual reporting. This practice has been freely acknowledged by *Washington Post* managing editor Philip Bennett.[19] He didn't mention, however, that a local Iraqi is pretty unlikely to have much journalistic training, but is highly likely to have his own political agenda.

In an October 2007 speech to military reporters, America's former top commander in Iraq, Ricardo Sanchez, opened his remarks with a devastating denunciation of press coverage of the war in Iraq: "What is clear to me is that you [reporters] are perpetuating the corrosive partisan politics that is destroying our country and killing our servicemembers who are at war. My assessment is that your profession, to some extent, has strayed from these ethical standards and allowed external agendas to manipulate what the American public sees on TV, what they read in our newspapers and what they see on the web. For some of you, just like some of our politicians, the truth is of little to no value if it does not fit your own preconceived notions, biases and agendas."[20] As if to prove Sanchez's point, the *New York Times'* article on his speech focused exclusively on his criticisms of the conduct of the war, not mentioning even once his blistering condemnation of the media.[21]

Oftentimes, ostensibly "objective" mainstream press reporters can't even hide their disdain for the Bush administration. After Dick Cheney accidentally shot a hunting companion, *Washington Post* White House correspondent Dana Milbank appeared on MSNBC to discuss the incident mockingly dressed in a hunting vest. When Karl Rove resigned as President Bush's advisor, members of the *Seattle Times* newsroom broke out in cheers.[22]

Can you rely on these kinds of people to bring you objective reporting about a war? They report, you decide.

Marines Say It Best

❝ What utter rubbish. ❞

—Eric Johnson, a veteran of Operation Iraqi Freedom, on the *Washington Post's* report of "intense anti-American sentiments" in the Iraqi city of Al Kut[23]

LIBERAL LUNACY:
"Because the media is dominated by for-profit businesses run largely by white males, they're really conservative and represent corporate interests."

This one is really a whopper. First, "corporate America" is not necessarily conservative. The federal government's antitrust lawsuit against Microsoft was encouraged by "corporate America" in the form of companies like Netscape.[24]

"Corporate America" has lobbied President Bush to raise steel tariffs, amnesty illegal immigrants, and increase regulations to fight global warming—not exactly conservative policies. Second, "corporate America" is hardly a monolithic entity. Liberals label anyone trying to make a profit—except the *New York Times* and tassled shoe-wearing trial lawyers—as part of "corporate America." This is false.

In fact, "corporate America" has lots of rabid liberals in its ranks. Investor extraordinaire Warren Buffet, CNN founder Ted Turner, and of course Bush-hating investor George Soros are all rich white males at the forefront of corporate America, but they're hardly card-carrying members of the Vast Right-Wing Conspiracy.

Liberals also fail to notice that the owners of the large media companies are not the ones producing and directing the content of television and print media. That's left to the liberals running the news desks and the lefty producers who decide which segments to air. Who decided to air the infamously false story alleging that President Bush shirked his National Guard duty during Vietnam? The president of CBS or Dan Rather and his longtime producer, Mary Mapes?

No liberal media bias? Then why did *Newsweek*, which had a tape of a young female intern discussing her affair with the president of the United States, decide not to go with the story? Maybe because it would reflect poorly on a Democratic president? (Instead, the Monica Lewinsky story was broken on the Internet by the Drudge Report.)

How can the press report politics objectively when 89 percent of the Washington bureau chiefs and reporters voted for Bill Clinton in 1992, while only 7 percent voted for George H. W. Bush? Only 43 percent of all Americans voted for Bill Clinton. More recently, an MSNBC study found that from 2004 through the beginning of the 2008 campaign, 125 journalists gave money to Democrats or liberal causes, while just sixteen donated to Republicans.[25] The media's conduct in the 2000 presidential election proves its liberal bias. Throughout election night, the networks publicly called states for Gore much sooner than they called states for Bush—even though the margin of victory was greater in the pro-Bush states than in the pro-Gore states. In *At Any Cost*, White House correspondent Bill Sammon reviewed the media's election night coverage. He found that Gore won Michigan by four points and was awarded the state by CNN the instant the first polls closed—even though voters in western Michigan still had another hour to vote. Bush won Ohio by the same margin, four points, but it took an hour and forty-five minutes for CNN to award the state to Bush. Gore won Illinois by twelve points and CNN named him the winner in one minute; Bush won Georgia by twelve points and CNN waited thirty-three minutes.[26]

Even more amazingly, Ann Coulter points out in *Slander* that "the Associated Press called Florida for Gore even though its own internal numbers had Bush winning—but refused to call Florida for Bush later in the evening when both its internal numbers and the [Voter News Services] numbers showed Bush the winner."[27]

And what about the 2004 presidential election? Same thing—liberal bias. Remember how the early exit polls, showing John Kerry winning, were broadcast loudly and widely? And, of course,

> **Mainstream Objectivity:**
>
> " I think most newspapermen by definition have to be liberal; if they're not liberal, by my definition of it, they can hardly be good newspapermen. "
>
> —Walter Cronkite, former CBS News anchor

the exit polling data, which was compiled by media organizations, turned out to be—surprise—not only wrong, but wrong in whose favor? John Kerry's.[29]

Keep this pattern of media bias in mind as you watch the results of the 2008 election roll in on election night.

LIBERAL LUNACY:
"But conservatives get hired to air their views in the major media."

Nope. When they get on at all, conservatives still have to go to the back of the bus. Sure, a handful of conservatives may get to appear on the major networks, but only as clearly labeled "conservative commentators"—not as plain ol' "objective reporters." You won't catch the major networks giving a conservative a slot to deliver hard, objective news.

So while George Stephanopoulos, one of Bill Clinton's top advisors, was hired by ABC as the host of *This Week,* conservatives such as Pat Buchanan and George Will are always boxed into "reserved" or "designated" conservative seats.

In her eye-opening book *Slander,* Ann Coulter supplies an impressive list of former Democratic staffers who appear on television as "objective" news purveyors. The list includes, among many others, NBC's Tim Russert, who worked for New York Democratic governor Mario Cuomo and Democratic senator Daniel Patrick Moynihan; CNN's Jeff Greenfield, who was a speechwriter for Democratic senator Bobby Kennedy and liberal New York mayor John Lindsay; and CNBC's Chris Matthews, who wrote speeches for Jimmy Carter and Reagan nemesis Tip O'Neill. PBS's Bill Moyers worked as President Lyndon Johnson's press secretary. None of these people are labeled "liberal" commentators; instead, they're presented as objective journalists. Conservatives don't get that kind of respect.

And, I ask, which former aide to President Bush has his own network television show? Karl Rove? Nope. Ari Fleischer? Uh-uh. The only former Bush administration official who has done well in the media after serving the president is Richard Clarke, with a bestselling book, a novel, and for a time, a regular gig as a columnist for the *New York Times Magazine*. Of course, Clarke broke ranks and sought to hurt Bush, so why wouldn't he be blessed with two great book deals and media adulation?

LIBERAL LUNACY:
"Even if journalists vote for Democrats, it does not mean that they unfairly report the news."

Let's talk about Rathergate. As you may recall, Rathergate arose during the heated 2004 presidential campaign, when Dan Rather and CBS News trotted out never-authenticated documents purporting to demonstrate that President Bush had performed poorly in the Air National Guard during the Vietnam War and that he received preferential treatment from his commanding officers. The story immediately began falling apart in the Pajama Media when bloggers determined that the typesettings of the documents did not exist in the 1970s (when the documents were supposedly created). Despite standing by the phony story for weeks, CBS News president Andrew Heyward finally admitted, "Based on what we now know, CBS News cannot prove that the documents are authentic, which is the only acceptable journalistic standard to justify using them in the report. We should not have used them. That was a mistake, which we deeply regret."

Think CBS was seeking to influence the 2004 election in favor of Kerry? Or did CBS News simply make an honest mistake by not adequately fact-checking what could have been the most important news story of the year? Well, given that bloggers sitting at home deconstructed the story in a matter of hours, one wonders why the powerful and wealthy CBS News failed to figure out these facts before airing the story. Perhaps CBS fact-checkers need to start wearing pajamas to work? Or better yet, just stay at home.

Another great example of how the liberal media reports stories biased against politically conservative views is how they report stories about gun control. The public policy organization Media Research Center conducted a study tracking for two years in the late 1990s how the major media reported on gun issues. The study found that of the 653 gun-policy stories broadcast, 357 stories tilted in favor of gun control while a mere thirty-six tilted against gun control That's an anti-gun bias of ten-to-one.[30] Likewise, John R. Lott, Jr. explained that in 2001, the three major television networks—NBC, CBS, and ABC—ran 190,000 words worth of gun crime stories on their morning and evening national news broadcasts. But they ran not a single story mentioning a private citizen using a gun to stop a crime. The print media was almost as biased: The *New York Times* ran 50,745 words on contemporaneous gun crimes, but only one short, 163-word story on guns used in self-defense. For *USA Today*, the tally was 5,660 words on gun crimes versus zero on defensive uses.[31]

More recently, the Culture and Media Institute found that in the first seven months of 2007, the three major networks broadcast 650 stories on firearm-related murders, and just two stories on guns used in self-defense. As the NRA commented, "Considering guns are used three to five times more often for self-defense than to commit a crime, this disproportion is staggering." [32] Staggering? Yes. Unexpected? Hardly.

VRWC TALKING POINTS

* Liberals hate FOX News because they can't stand the existence of a single cable TV channel that won't parrot the liberal agenda.

* Liberals' demand to bring back the Fairness Doctrine is really an attempt to shut down talk radio, where liberals can't compete with conservatives.

* The *New York Times* has a decades-long history of liberal bias that continues today.

* Mainstream newspapers infuse their reporting of the Iraq War with liberal bias.

* Reporting decisions in the mainstream media are not made by corporate bosses, but by liberal editors and news producers.

* On television, liberals are trusted as objective reporters and are given positions running news shows, while conservatives are specifically labeled as partisans.

* As shown by everything from Rathergate to the reporting of election results, reporters allow their liberal bias to affect their reporting.

Economist John Maynard Keynes once said, "The ideas of economists and political philosophers, both when they are right and when they are wrong, are more powerful than is commonly understood. Indeed, the world is ruled by little else. Practical men, who believe themselves to be quite exempt from any intellectual influences, are usually the slaves of some defunct economist. Madmen in authority, who hear voices in the air, are distilling their frenzy from some academic scribbler of a few years back."

Who are the economists, political philosophers, and academic scribblers of the modern conservative movement? There are many, and the list is growing.

This book is the product of reading conservative authors, attending lectures and debates, watching political shows on television or listening to them on the radio, and my own personal experiences debating liberals in New York City and on television. Because the *Handbook* is not intended to be a definitive work on any of the issues addressed, here is a list of resources and information that I have found helpful in staying abreast of Conspiracy developments.

INSPIRATIONAL INDIVIDUALS

In addition to conservative politicians and their advisors, there are hundreds of intelligent and articulate conservative commentators. Here is a list of those individuals whom I have found particularly interesting and persuasive. I pay attention when I see articles by these folks and when they appear on my television. On particular points, these commentators may disagree with me and I with them. That's okay. Often, you can learn much from listening to and communicating with those with whom you disagree.

Glenn Beck, conservative talk radio personality and host of the *Glenn Beck* news show on CNN Headline News.

Bill Bennett, former U.S. Secretary of Education, bestselling author, and head of the public policy group Empower America. Bennett always offers an intelligent view, though he is particularly good on education and foreign policy issues.

Neal Boortz, entertaining radio talk-show host and bestselling author of *The Fair Tax Book: Saying Goodbye to the Income Tax and the IRS.*

Judge Robert Bork, former federal judge, professor of law, bestselling author, and scholar at the American Enterprise Institute. Bork's views on the state of American law are particularly insightful.

Brent Bozell, president of the Media Research Center and one of the nation's foremost experts on liberal bias in the media.

Patrick Buchanan, longtime columnist, former presidential candidate, telegenic talk-show host, and articulate defender of the America First movement.

William F. Buckley Jr., raconteur, founder of the influential *National Review* magazine, bestselling author, and one of the earliest conservatives on television with PBS's *Firing Line.*

Kellyanne Conway, founder, president, and CEO of the Washington, D.C.–based "The Polling Company," conservative commentator, and one of the "Fifty Most Powerful Women in Politics," according to *Ladies' Home Journal.*

Ann Coulter, perhaps the second most famous woman (after Hillary) in American politics today. Coulter is an attorney, bestselling author, legal correspondent for *Human Events,* and a conservative diva who sets the standard against which all other conservative commentators should be compared.

T. Kenneth Cribb, Jr., president of the Intercollegiate Studies Institute and of the Collegiate Network. He previously served as President Reagan's top domestic policy advisor.

Monica Crowley, successful author, Richard Nixon scholar, and radio show host.

Matt Drudge, founder and operator of the Drudge Report (www.drudgereport.com), the nation's best web site for the most up-to-date news and political gossip.

Dinesh D'Souza, research fellow at the Hoover Institution, bestselling author, true American success story, and definitely a person with whom you would want to serve on a college Republican newspaper.

Michelle Easton, president of the Clare Boothe Luce Policy Institute and veteran soldier in the battle to improve America's education standards.

Lee Edwards, chief historian of the conservative movement who has published over fifteen books about conservative leaders and institutions. He is also chairman of the Victims of Communism Memorial foundation.

Larry Elder, Los Angeles–based radio talk-show host known as the "Sage from South Central" who debunks popular liberal myths every day, as well as in his excellent book, *The Ten Things You Can't Say in America.*

Richard Epstein, law professor, author, and clearly one of the smartest people in the world, with the ability to explain theoretically yet clearly the most complicated legal and political issues.

Mallory Factor, chairman of the Free Enterprise Fund and co-founder of the influential Monday Meeting in New York City.

Don Feder, columnist, author, radio talk-show host and all-around talented conservative pundit.

Steve Forbes, editor and president of the free market–oriented *Forbes* magazine and former presidential candidate who brought the idea of a "flat rate income tax" into the mainstream.

John Fund, intelligent conservative pundit who writes editorials for the *Wall Street Journal* and collaborated with Rush Limbaugh on the bestseller *The Way Things Ought to Be.*

Frank Gaffney, founder of the Center for Security Policy and an insightful commentator on American foreign policy and defense issues.

Robert George, standup comedian and editorial writer for the *New York Post.*

John Gizzi, political editor of *Human Events.* Gizzi is the ultimate insider on Capitol Hill with an almanac's mastery of politics.

Jonah Goldberg, Lucianne's son and a darn funny writer for *National Review Online.*

Lucianne Goldberg, founder of the popular web site www.lucianne.com, former New York literary agent, mom of Jonah, and hated by liberals (but loved by conservatives) for her role in helping prove Bill Clinton's felonious perjury in the Paula Jones/Monica Lewinsky affairs.

Sean Hannity, media superstar, radio talk-show host, bestselling author, co-host of FOX News Channel's *Hannity & Colmes*, and host of *Hannity's America* on the same channel.

Victor Davis Hanson, prominent professor emeritus, prolific author, and columnist for *National Review*.

Mark Helprin, author and excellent writer for the Claremont Institute and the *Wall Street Journal*.

Hugh Hewitt, author, blogger, and nationally syndicated talk-show host.

James Higgins, co-founder of the Monday Meeting in New York City.

David Horowitz, successful author, intellectual bomb-thrower, brilliant political strategist, and a man who understands the application of the "art of war" to politics and how Republicans should use it.

Laura Ingraham, attorney, bestselling author, media star, and host of her own nationally syndicated radio show.

Terence Jeffrey, nationally syndicated columnist and frequent defender of the Right on cable news.

Elizabeth Kantor, author of *The Politically Incorrect Guide™ to English and American Literature* and head of the Conservative Book Club, the best source of conservative books.

William Kristol, author and editor of the *Weekly Standard* magazine. Kristol is an influential conservative in print, in the lecture hall, and on the airwaves.

David Kopel, author and research director at the Independence Institute, and author of numerous outstanding pieces explaining why guns are good.

Michael Ledeen, author and scholar at the American Enterprise Institute. Ledeen understands what it will take to destroy international terrorism and its supporters.

Leonard Leo, executive vice president of the Federalist Society, the nation's largest organization of conservative lawyers, and adviser to President George W. Bush on judicial nominations.

David Limbaugh, attorney, bestselling author, and nationally syndicated columnist whose book *Persecution: How Liberals are Waging War against Christianity*, is an eye-opener—even for Ayn Rand libertarians.

Rush Limbaugh, mega media superstar, bestselling author, and radio host who has single-handedly given more liberals heart attacks than tobacco, fatty foods, and alcohol combined.

John R. Lott, Jr., statistician and economics professor. Lott is the author of *Freedomnomics*, a rousing defense of the free market and rebuke to assorted government interventionists.

Rich Lowry, editor of *National Review* and author of the now-definitive history of the Clinton era, *Legacy: Paying the Price for the Clinton Years*.

Michelle Malkin, bestselling author, nationally syndicated columnist, frequent Fox News commentator, Clare Booth Luce Policy Institute's 2006 Woman of the Year, and prominent member of Pajamas Media. Read her blog at www.michellemalkin.com.

Manuel Miranda, chairman of the Third Branch Conference, former counsel to Senate Majority Leader Bill Frist, and the attorney who revealed memos prepared by Senate Democrats, describing their unfair targeting of George W. Bush's judicial nominees.

Stephen Moore, economist, member of the *Wall Street Journal* editorial board, and former president of the Club for

Growth. Moore is an articulate, passionate spokesman and political activist for less government, free markets, and tax cuts.

Dick Morris, yes, Morris worked for Bill Clinton, but his political analysis on the FOX News Channel is second to none. Morris has been a strong critic of Hillary Rodham Clinton, thus earning him at least an honorable mention from the VRWC.

Joel Mowbray, syndicated columnist and author of *Dangerous Diplomacy: How the State Department Threatens America's Security.* Mowbray shocked the nation with his discovery that all of the fifteen visa applications submitted by the 9/11 hijackers should have been rejected.

Deroy Murdock, influential New York–based nationally syndicated columnist and columnist for *National Review Online.*

Charles Murray, author of several influential books, including the groundbreaking *Losing Ground,* which showed how government welfare programs actually hurt America's poor.

Benjamin Netanyahu, the most eloquent and intelligent defender of Israel and advocate of the strategy of destroying terrorists instead of pandering to them.

Grover Norquist, Republican activist extraordinaire, whose work as president for Americans for Tax Reform is just part of his overall plan to make the Republican Party into the majority party for decades to come.

Oliver North, war hero, bestselling author, columnist, television and radio star, and almost-U.S. senator. Simply put, North is a great American hero.

Walter Olson, author, Manhattan Institute scholar, and founder of the influential website www.overlawyered.com, a fantastic resource for research, facts, and anecdotes about how the law and lawyers are dragging down America.

Bill O'Reilly, bestselling author and straight-talking, common sense–advocating host of top-ranked television show *The O'Reilly Factor.*

Richard Poe, bestselling author of *Seven Myths of Gun Control* and founder of the blogsite www.richardpoe.com.

Ron Robinson, president of the Young America's Foundation who leads the challenging campaign to spread conservative thought in academia.

Evan Sayet, the rarest of breeds—a conservative standup comic. Also a conservative activist, public speaker, and former television writer and producer.

Jay Sekulow, chief counsel to the American Center for Law & Justice and an accomplished Supreme Court advocate.

Mark Skousen, unique and entertaining free market economist, author of *Investing in One Lesson,* and editor of the financial newsletter "Mark Skousen's Forecasts and Strategies."

Thomas Sowell, author, columnist, and fellow at the Hoover Institution. Sowell's columns and books are always must-reads.

John Stossel, a free market libertarian and gadfly to the liberal media who anchors *The John Stossel Specials* for ABC News and frequently appears on ABC's *20/20.* Stossel's programs are must-sees and are always worth watching—even taping.

Phylis Schlafly, one of the most extraordinary women of the twentieth century, who single-handedly led the movement to stop the liberals' Holy Grail, the Equal Rights Amendment.

R. Emmett "Bob" Tyrrell, Jr., founder and editor-in-chief of *The American Spectator* magazine and author of *Madame Hillary: The Dark Road to the White House.*

Richard Viguerie, pioneer of direct mail fundraising who was instrumental in consolidating the conservative movement.

Eugene Volokh, young and energetic legal intellectual, prolific writer, and professor of law at UCLA Law School.

George Will, author, columnist, and longtime conservative pundit on Sunday morning talk shows.

Walter Williams, professor, economist, author, columnist, and occasional host of Rush Limbaugh's radio show. Williams's writings are always must-reads.

Tom Winter, long-time conservative activist who is editor-in-chief of *Human Events*, first vice chairman of the American Conservative Union, and treasurer of the Conservative Victory Fund.

CONSERVATIVE THINK TANKS AND ORGANIZATIONS

Conservatives have experienced so much political success over the last decade in part because of their ability to circumvent the information flow gushing from the liberal-controlled media, public schools, and universities. And how have conservatives been able to evade these liberal monoliths? Two major reasons are the rise of the Internet and the ever-growing import of outstanding conservative think tanks. The combination of research and analysis from conservative think tanks, with their ability to use the Internet and cable news to communicate their opinions to the public, provides critical information to conservative politicians, conservative media folks, and even conservative college students under siege at liberal universities. No more are Americans forced to choose between the "moderate" liberals at NBC News and the "socialists" of National Public Radio.

Over the years, I have found the following conservative and libertarian organizations and think tanks to offer many intelligent arguments, facts, and opinions against liberalism. For anyone interested in learning more about how to defeat liberals, familiarity with the following groups and their websites is invaluable.

Alliance for Marriage, *www.allianceformarriage.org.* Group dedicated to the fight to preserve traditional marriage.

American Center for Law & Justice, *www.aclj.org.* Organization devoted to advancing religious and constitutional freedom.

American Conservative Union, *www.conservative.org.* Longtime grass-roots conservative political organization that sponsors the annual CPAC convention and supports capitalism, a strong national defense, traditional moral values, and interpreting the Constitution according to the original intent of the Framers.

American Enterprise Institute, *www.aei.org.* Think tank devoted to free markets, limited government, and strong national defense.

American Family Association, *www.afa.net.* Nonprofit organization that aims to strengthen family values, especially in the entertainment industry.

America's Future Foundation, *www.americasfuture.org.* Organization dedicated to enhancing conservative, libertarian, and free-market ideals among young, post-college professionals.

American Life League, *www.all.org.* Outstanding and influential pro-life organization.

Americans for Tax Reform, *www.atr.org.* Influential anti-tax organization run by grass-roots organizer extraordinaire Grover Norquist.

Atlantic Legal Foundation, *www.atlanticlegal.org.* New York–based public interest law firm advancing the cause of limited government, free enterprise, and sound (i.e., not junk) science.

Capital Research Center, *www.capitalresearch.org.* Excellent organization that identifies private alternatives to government entitlement programs and monitors non-profits, labor unions, and corporate philanthropy.

CATO Institute, *www.cato.org.* Leading libertarian think tank advocating less government, free markets, and the protection of property rights.

Center for Individual Rights, *www.cir-usa.org.* Leading conservative public interest law firm.

Center for the Study of Popular Culture, *www.cspc.org.* Scholar David Horowitz's organization dedicated to advancing the cause of America and conservatism; publishes the influential *FrontPage Magazine* at *www.frontpagemag.com.*

Citizens Against Government Waste, *www.cagw.org.* An organization dedicated to eliminating waste, mismanagement, and inefficiency in the federal government.

Citizens United, *www.citizensunited.org.* Educational, advocacy, and grassroots organization.

Clare Boothe Luce Policy Institute, *www.cblpi.org.* Organization devoted to encouraging conservative women to embrace leadership roles in our nation's future.

Club for Growth, *www.clubforgrowth.org.* Political organization devoted to helping elect antitax, limited government, and pro-economic growth politicians adhering to the economic views espoused by President Ronald Reagan.

Competitive Enterprise Institute, *www.cei.org.* Think tank devoted to free enterprise and limited government.

Concerned Women for America, *www.cwfa.org.* Women's organization dedicated to advancing public policies consistent with Biblical principles. It supports traditional families, the sanctity of life, education reform, religious liberty, and American sovereignty over international bodies such as the United Nations.

Defenders of Property Rights, *www.yourpropertyrights. org.* Public interest law firm dedicated to preserving individual property rights and restoring the Fifth Amendment's Takings Clause in America.

Eagle Forum, *www.eagleforum.org.* Indispensable organization led by Phyllis Schlafly that supports U.S. sovereignty, traditional families, the free market, and everything else good about America.

Empower America, *www.empoweramerica.org.* Bill Bennett's organization dedicated to educational reform, a strong national defense, free markets, and Social Security reform.

Ethics and Public Policy Center, *www.eppc.org.* An active scholarly group reinforcing the bond between traditional values and good policy.

Family Research Council, *www.frc.org.* Washington D.C. organization dedicated to reaffirming traditional Judeo-Christian values.

Federalist Society for Law and Public Policy Studies, *www.fed-soc.org.* The premier organization in the nation for conservative attorneys who believe that judges should interpret, but not make, laws.

Fidelis, *www.fidelis.org.* Pro-life and pro-family Catholic advocacy group.

Focus on the Family, *www.family.org.* Led by Dr. James Dobson, this massive Colorado-based organization is on the forefront of the marriage and culture wars.

Foundation for Economics Education (FEE), *www. fee.org.* The nation's oldest organization dedicated to advancing free markets, limited government, and free trade.

Foundation for Individual Rights in Education (FIRE), *www.thefire.org.* Dedicated to ridding America's universities of the censorship arising from political correctness and radical liberalism.

Free Congress Foundation, *www.freecongress.org.* A politically and culturally conservative influential organization.

FreedomWorks, *www.freedomworks.org.* Grassroots organization pursuing lower taxes, less government, and more freedom. Led by former U.S. House Majority leader Dick Armey.

Free Enterprise Fund, *www.freeenterprisefund.org.* One of the nation's most prominent advocacy groups devoted to encouraging economic prosperity through free markets, lower taxes, and less government.

Gun Owners of America, *www.gunowners.org.* Aggressive pro-gun rights organization.

Heartland Institute, *www.heartland.org.* Chicago-based organization advocating school choice, free market solutions to environmental issues, privatization, and deregulation; publisher of the outstanding publication *Environment and Climate News,* which advocates common-sense environmentalism.

Heritage Foundation, *www.heritage.org.* Powerful and influential conservative think tank.

Home School Legal Defense Association, *www.hslda.org.* The largest national home schooling group fights for educational freedom and parental rights.

Hoover Institution, *www-hoover.stanford.edu.* One of the most influential intellectual institutions in the world, with preeminent scholars such as Victor Davis Hanson and Thomas Sowell.

Independent Women's Forum, *www.iwf.org.* A conservative antidote to liberal feminists, the IWF proves that truly strong, smart, and independent woman need not toe America's radical liberal agenda.

Institute for Humane Studies, *www.theihs.org.* Located at George Mason University in Virginia, the IHS helps college and graduate students learn about free markets and individual liberty.
Institute for Justice, *www.ij.org.* Free market–oriented public interest law firm well known for successfully litigating for school choice programs and against silly government regulations.
Institute on Religion and Public Life, *www.firstthings.com.* Led by Richard John Neuhaus, an organization devoted to conservative and neoconservative religious philosophy and publishers of the magazine *First Things.*
Intercollegiate Studies Institute (ISI), *www.isi.org.* Works to educate students about the classical foundations of individual liberty.
Landmark Legal Foundation, *www.landmarklegal.org.* Well-known free market conservative-oriented public interest law firm.
Leadership Institute, *www.leadershipinstitute.org.* Premier organization dedicated to training young conservatives to be future leaders of the conservative movement.
Manhattan Institute for Policy Research, *www.manhattan-institute.org.* Longtime influential conservative think tank based in New York City. The Manhattan Institute offers an impressive array of scholars articulating conservative and free market solutions to urban problems.
Media Research Center, *www.mediaresearch.org.* "America's media watchdog" devoted to documenting the liberal bias in the mainstream media.
National Center for Public Policy Research, *www.nationalcenter.org.* Research and communications organization supporting a strong national defense and free markets.

National Federation of Independent Business, *www.nfib.com.* The political lobbying organization on behalf of America's small businesses, for free enterprise and free markets, and against intrusive government interference in the economy.

National Legal Center for Public Interest, *www.nlcpi.org.* A law foundation dedicated to fostering knowledge about the law and justice in a society committed to free enterprise, property rights, and individual rights.

National Rifle Association, *www.nra.org.* One of the most influential and powerful organizations (at least I hope so) in the nation, with 3 million members dedicated to preserving the Second Amendment and the individual right to own guns.

National Right to Life Committee, *www.nrlc.org.* Pro-life organization founded in 1973 shortly after the *Roe v. Wade* decision.

National Taxpayers Union, *www.ntu.org.* Influential anti-tax and limited government organization.

Pacific Legal Foundation, *www.pacificlegal.org.* West Coast–based public interest law firm advancing causes of free enterprise and individual property rights while fighting intrusive government regulations and policies based upon "junk" environmental science.

Priests for Life, *www.priestsforlife.org.* An active and outspoken pro-life association of Catholic priests.

60 Plus Association, *www.60plus.org.* Seniors' advocacy group supportive of applying notions of free enterprise, less government, and less taxes approach to seniors' issues.

Southeastern Legal Foundation, *www.southeasternlegal.org.* Atlanta-based public interest law firm advancing the causes of limited government, individual economic freedom, and the free enterprise system.

Washington Legal Foundation, *www.wlf.org*. A public-interest legal center that uses lawsuits and publications to advance the causes of free enterprise, property rights, a strong national defense, and a fair civil and criminal justice system.

Young America's Foundation, *www.yaf.org*. Based in Herndon, Virginia, and at the Reagan Ranch in Santa Barbara, California, the foundation runs the largest outreach program to ensure that young Americans understand and are inspired by freedom, strong defense, and traditional values.

MAGAZINES AND NEWSPAPERS

American Enterprise

American Spectator

America's First Freedom

City Journal

Claremont Review of Books

Commentary

Conservative Chronicle

First Things

Freeman: Ideas on Liberty

Human Events

Imprimis

Intercollegiate Review

National Review

New York Post

New York Sun

Reason Magazine

Wall Street Journal

Washington Times

Weekly Standard

INTERNET NEWS SITES AND WEBLOGS

Drudge Report (*www.drudgereport.com*)

Free Republic (*www.freerepublic.com*)

Frontpagemag (*www.frontpagemag.com*)

Hugh Hewitt (*www.hughhewitt.com*)

Hot Air (*www.hotair.com*)

Human Events (http://www.humanevents.com)

Instapundit (*www.instapundit.com*)

Jihadwatch (*www.jihadwatch.com*)

Little Green Footballs (*www.littlegreenfootballs.com*)

Michelle Malkin (*www.michellemalkin.com*)

National Review (*http://corner.nationalreview.com*)
Newsmax (*www.newsmax.com*)
Powerline (*www.powerlineblog.com*)
Real Clear Politics (*www.realclearpolitics.com*)
Red State (*www.redstate.com*)
Townhall (*www.townhall.com*)
Worldnetdaily (*www.worldnetdaily.com*)

RECOMMENDED BOOKS

Avery, Dennis and Singer, S. Fred, *Unstoppable Global Warming: Every 1,500 Years* (Lanham, MD: Roman and Littlefield Publishers, 2007). Two professors argue convincingly that global warming is a natural phenomenon.

Bailey, Ronald (editor), *Global Warming and Other Eco-Myths: How the Environmental Movement Uses False Science to Scare Us to Death* (New York: Prima Publishing, 2002). An excellent book written by many experts who debunk numerous myths about the purportedly "dangerous state of the environment."

Bastiat, Frederic, *The Law: The Classic Blueprint for a Just Society* (Irvington, NY: Foundation for Economic Education, 1998). First published in 1850 by the author, who explains in this long essay how to think about individual liberty and government in a free society.

Bennett, William J., *Why We Fight—Moral Clarity and the War on Terrorism* (Washington, D.C.: Regnery, 2003). Justifies both the war on terror and the war in Iraq.

Biswnanger, Harry, (editor) *The Ayn Rand Lexicon: Objectivism from A to Z* (New York: Penguin, 1986.)

Blankley, Tony, *The West's Last Chance* (Washington, D.C.: Regnery, 2005). Former editorial page editor of the *Washington*

Times writes that Eurabia poses a greater threat to the U.S. than did Nazi Germany.

Blyth, Myrna, *Spin Sisters: How the Women of the Media Sell Unhappiness and Liberalism to American Women* (New York: St. Martin's Press, 2004). Former editor in chief of *Ladies Home Journal* describes "the negative message of victimization and unhappiness that bombards women."

Bolick, Clint, *Voucher Wars: Waging the Legal Battle over School Choice* (Washington, D.C.: Cato Institute, 2003). The case for school choice discussed in the context of Bolick's litigation on behalf of the cause.

Boortz, Neal, *The Fair Tax Book: Saying Goodbye to the Income Tax and the IRS* (New York: HarperCollins, 2005). Explains the heavy drag on the American economy from taxes and provides a plan to eliminate the income tax and the IRS.

Bork, Robert H., *Coercing Virtue: The Worldwide Rule of Judges* (Washington, D.C.: AEI, 2003). How judges in the United States and abroad seek to take decision-making from the democratic and political processes.

Bork, Robert H., *Slouching Towards Gomorrah—Modern Liberalism and American Decline* (New York: ReganBooks/Harper-Collins, 1996). Chronicles the debasement of American culture.

Bork, Robert H., *The Tempting of America—The Political Seduction of the Law* (New York: Simon & Schuster, 1990). Explains the dangers of judges making law and usurping the democratic political process.

Clare Boothe Luce Policy Institute. *Great American Conservative Women* (Washington, D.C.: CBLPI, 2002). Collection of speeches from prominent conservative women such as Dr. Laura Schlessinger, Jeane Kirkpratrick, Ann Coulter, Star Parker, Linda Chavez, and Phyllis Schlafly.

Coulter, Ann, *High Crimes and Misdeameanors: The Case Against Bill Clinton* (Washington, D.C.: Regnery, 1999). Why Bill Clinton deserved to be impeached.

Coulter, Ann, *How to Talk to a Liberal (If You Must)* (New York: Crown, 2005). Collection of Coulter's most entertaining columns.

Coulter, Ann, *If Democrats had any Brains, They'd be Republicans* (New York: Crown Forum, 2007). Coulter's latest thoughts on Democrats and the general state of the union.

Coulter, Ann, *Slander: Liberal Lies about the American Right* (New York: Crown, 2002). How liberals control the mass media and advance liberalism by lying about conservatives.

Coulter, Ann, *Treason: Liberal Treachery from the Cold War to the War on Terrorism* (New York: Crown Forum, 2003). How liberals keep siding against the United States.

Courtois, Stephane, et al., *The Black Book of Communism: Crimes, Terror, Repression* (Cambridge, MA: Harvard University Press, 1997). A tome analyzing the archives of the former Soviet bloc and showing how Soviet communism led to terror, murder, and repression; in short, a vindication of Reagan's belief that the Soviet Union was an "evil empire."

Crier, Catherine, *The Case against Lawyers* (New York: Broadway Books, 2002). An eloquent indictment of the current criminal and civil justice systems.

Dershowitz, Alan, *The Case for Israel* (New York: John Wiley & Sons, 2003). Dershowitz puts his lawyerly skills to good use in making the case for Israel and battling back the typical anti-Israel arguments.

D'Souza, Dinesh, *Letters to a Young Conservative* (New York: Basic Books, 2002). An excellent primer on conservative thought, written in the thoroughly enjoyable style of C. S. Lewis's *The Screwtape Letters.*

D'Souza, Dinesh, *Ronald Reagan: How an Ordinary Man Became an Extraordinary Leader* (New York: Simon & Schuster, 1997). A fun and informative discussion of the man who won the Cold War and revived America's greatness.

D'Souza, Dinesh, *What's So Great About America* (Washington, D.C.: Regnery, 2002). Defends the U.S. against liberal attacks by multiculturalists and anti-American liberals.

D'Souza, Dinesh, *What's So Great About Christianity* (Washington, D.C.: Regnery, 2007). Comprehensive rebuttal of trendy atheist and leftist claims that Christianity is a leading source of oppression and warfare.

Elder, Larry, *Showdown: Confronting Bias, Lies, and Special Interests that Divide America* (Irvine, CA: Griffin, 2003). A continued attack on liberal myths.

Elder, Larry, *The Ten Things You Can't Say In America* (New York: St. Martin's Press, 2000). A fun attack on popular liberal myths.

Forbes, Steve, *Flat Tax Revolution: Using a Postcard to Abolish the IRS* (Washington, D.C.: Regnery, 2005). The best, most comprehensive argument for the flat tax.

Friedman, Milton, *Capitalism and Freedom* (Chicago: University of Chicago Press, 1962). An eloquent defense of free markets and individual economic freedom, written in a more scholarly style than *Free to Choose.*

Friedman, Milton and Rose Friedman, *Free to Choose: A Personal Statement* (New York: Harcourt, 1980). An eloquent defense of free markets and individual economic freedom.

Furchtgott-Roth, Diana and Christine Stolba, *Women's Figures: An Illustrated Guide to the Economic Progress of Women in America* (Washington, D.C.: The AEI Press and Independent Women's Forum, 1999). An outstanding resource and treasure trove of key facts and statistics about the status of women in America.

Gabriel, Brigitte, *Because They Hate: A Survivor of Islamic Terror Warns America* (New York: St. Martin's Press, 2006). A Christian Arab warns of the threat Islamic radicals pose to America.

Gibson, John, *The War on Christmas: How the Liberal Plot to Ban the Sacred Christian Holiday Is Worse Than You Thought* (New York: Sentinel, 2005). Describes the anti-Christmas campaign in which liberal activist, ACLU fanatics, and Democratic politicians now engage.

Goldberg, Bernard, *Bias: A CBS Insider Exposes How the Media Distort the News* (Washington, D.C.: Regnery, 2002). An insightful and eye-opening account of the career dangers of straying from the liberal agenda as a reporter for CBS News.

Hannity, Sean, *Let Freedom Ring: Winning the War of Liberty over Liberalism* (New York: ReganBooks, 2002). A clear and concise argument against liberalism in a world at war with terrorism.

Hayek, F. A., *The Road to Serfdom* (Chicago: University of Chicago Press, 1944). The case against the rise of big-government socialism in the twentieth century.

Hirsi Ali, Ayaan, *Infidel* (New York: Free Press, 2007). Autobiography of Somali-born former Dutch MP who faced continual death threats for criticizing Islam.

Horowitz, David, *How the Left Undermined America's Security* (Washington, D.C.: Center for the Study of Popular Culture, 2002). A great, concise, and detailed case about how liberals and their policies undermined America's national security, leading to 9/11.

Horowitz, David, *How to Beat the Democrats And Other Subversive Ideas* (Dallas: Spence Publishing Company, 2002). A clear vision about how conservatives can win at the ballot box by a true political genius.

Horowitz, David, *The Professors: The 101 Most Dangerous Academics in America* (Washington, D.C.: Regnery, 2006). A shocking book about radical anti-American liberals who dwell on America's college campuses, seeking to indoctrinate students into the faith of liberalism.

Howard, Philip, *The Death of Common Sense: How Law is Suffocating America* (New York: Random House, 1994). A great book about how regulations suffocate American business and American life.

Huber, Peter W., *Hard Green: Saving The Environment From the Environmentalists—A Conservative Manifesto* (New York: Basic Books, 1999). Makes the case for free market environmentalism.

Huber, Peter W., *Liability: The Legal Revolution and its Consequences* (New York: Basic Books, 1988). Explains how tort law is changing America.

Ingraham, Laura, *The Hillary Trap: Looking For Power In All The Wrong Places* (New York: Hyperion, 2000). The case against Hillary Rodham Clinton and her vision of women in America.

Ingraham, Laura, *Shut Up & Sing: How Elites from Hollywood, Politics, and the UN Are Subverting America* (Washington, D.C.: Regnery, 2003). A fun and irreverent look at liberal elites in all their forms.

Ingraham, Laura. *Power to the People* (Washington, D.C.: Regnery, 2007). An action plan for reclaiming America from the Left.

Kaplan, Lawrence and William Kristol, *The War Over Iraq: Saddam's Tyranny and America's Mission* (San Francisco: Encounter Books, 2003). A scholarly yet accessible case for invading Iraq.

Kent, Phil, *The Dark Side of Liberalism: Unchaining the Truth* (Augusta, GA: Harbor House, 2003). A clear and concise attack on liberalism.

LaPierre, Wayne and James Jay Baker, *Shooting Straight: Telling The Truth About Guns In America* (Washington, D.C.: Regnery, 2002). Defends the Second Amendment and gun ownership in America against liberals seeking to use the 9/11 attacks to confiscate guns.

Ledeen, Michael, *The War Against the Terror Masters: Why It Happened. Where We Are Now. How We'll Win* (New York: St. Martin's Press, 2002). A detailed account of how Middle Eastern nations provide terrorist organizations with the infrastructure needed to carry out terrorist attacks on civilization.

Levin, Mark R., *Men in Black* (Washington, D.C.: Regnery, 2005). Explains how liberal judicial activists harm America.

Lewis, Bernard, *The Crisis of Islam: Holy War and Unholy Terror* (New York: Random House, 2003). A great, clear explanation of the Islamic world and its views of the Western world.

Lieberman, Myron, *The Teacher Unions: How they Sabotage Educational Reform and Why* (San Francisco: Encounter Books, 2000). Describes the growth of teacher unions and how they work to thwart educational reform.

Limbaugh, David, *Persecution: How Liberals Are Waging War Against Christianity* (Washington, D.C.: Regnery, 2003). The bestselling book detailing how liberals attack Christianity.

Limbaugh, Rush, *The Way Things Ought To Be* (New York: Pocket Books, 1992). An irreverent, persuasive, and fact-filled case against liberalism.

Lomborg, Bjørn, *The Skeptical Environmentalist: Measuring the Real State of the World* (Cambridge: Cambridge University Press, 2001). If you read only one book about liberal environmentalist myths and the falsity of their prognostications about the state of the world, this is the book; no book better debunks the flawed science and flawed record of liberal doomsday predictions than this one, written by a Danish statistics professor.

Lomborg, Bjørn, *Cool It: The Skeptical Environmentalist's Guide to Global Warming* (New York: Knopf, 2007). Follow-up to *The Skeptical Environmentalist* that rebuts the latest faulty science and false claims of Al Gore and other global warming alarmists.

Lott, John R., Jr., *The Bias Against Guns: Why Almost Everything You've Heard About Gun Control Is Wrong* (Washington, D.C.: Regnery, 2003). How guns save lives and how the media refuse to report this fact.

Lott, John R., Jr., *More Guns, Less Crime: Understanding Crime and Gun Control Laws* (Chicago: University of Chicago Press,

1998). The famous statistical case for encouraging widespread gun ownership in America.

Lott, John R., *Freedomnomics: Why the Free Market Works and Other Half-Baked Theories Don't* (Washington, D.C.: Regnery, 2007). Lott skewers free market skeptics, explaining why government intrusion inevitably makes problems worse.

Luttrell, Marcus, *Lone Survivor: The Eyewitness Account of Operation Redwing and the Lost Heroes of Seal Team 10* (New York: Little, Brown, and Company, 2007). Heart-pounding first-person account of heroic Navy Seals battling the Taliban.

MacDonald, Heather, *Are Cops Racist?* (Chicago: Ivan R. Dee, 2003) Debunks the myth of "racial profiling" in America.

Malkin, Michelle, *Unhinged: Exposing Liberals Gone Wild* (Washington, D.C.: Regnery, 2005). Provides support and numerous illustrations about how the American Left has gone bonkers over its status in contemporary America.

Moe, Terry M., *Schools, Vouchers, and the American Public* (Washington, D.C.: Brookings Institution Press, 2001). Explains how the American public views school voucher proposals.

Moore, Stephen and Julian L. Simon, *It's Getting Better All the Time: The Greatest Trends of the Last 100 Years* (Washington, D.C.: Cato Institute, 2000). An outstanding resource full of invaluable statistics and data showing the amazing contributions to humankind the U.S.'s devotion to free markets and individual liberty has endowed upon this society.

Murray, Charles, *Losing Ground: American Social Policy 1950–1980* (New York: HarperCollins, 1984). The famous case against government welfare.

Novak, Robert, *The Prince of Darkness: 50 Years Reporting in Washington.* Memoir of the veteran conservative journalist and commentator.

O'Beirne, Kate, *Women Who Make the World Worse and How Their Radical Feminist Assault Is Ruining Our Schools, Family, Military, and Sports* (New York: Sentinel, 2005). Well-written and intelligent attack on modern-day feminism.

O'Sullivan, John, *The President, the Pope, and the Prime Minister: Three who Changed the World* (Washington, D.C.: Regnery, 2006). Appreciative account of the role played by Ronald Reagan, John Paul II, and Margaret Thatcher in bringing down communism and reinvigorating western civilization.

Ponurru, Ramesh, *The Party of Death: The Democrats, the Media, the Courts, and the Disregard for Human Life* (Washington, D.C.: Regnery, 2006). A cogent study of the Left's refusal to choose life.

Read, Leonard, *Anything That's Peaceful* (Irvington, NY: Foundation for Economic Education, 1998). Originally published in 1964, Read explains in easy-to-understand language the libertarian, free market view of the economic world.

Reagan, Ronald, *The Reagan Diaries* (New York: Harper-Collins, 2007). Insightful diary kept by the great man himself during his tenure as president.

Sammon, Bill, *At Any Cost: How Al Gore Tried to Steal the Election,* (Washington, D.C.: Regnery, 2001). A straightforward account of how the liberal media and Al Gore tried to steal Florida from George Bush.

Sammon, Bill, *Fighting Back* (Washington, D.C.: Regnery, 2002). How the Bush administration led the nation after 9/11.

Sammon, Bill, *Strategery* (Washington, D.C.: Regnery, 2006). How President Bush is defeating terrorists, outwitting Democrats, and confounding the mainstream media.

Sammon, Bill, *The Evangelical President* (Washington, D.C.: Regnery, 2007). An intimate look at the Bush presidency from 2005 to 2007.

Sanera, Michael and Jane S. Shaw, *Facts, Not Fear: Teaching Children about the Environment* (Washington, D.C.: Regnery, 1999). A valuable primer on environmental issues from a non-hysterical, non-"sky is falling" view.

Schlafly, Phyllis, *Feminist Fantasies* (Dallas: Spence Publishing Company, 2003). Essays articulating the case against radical feminism, with an outstanding foreword by Ann Coulter describing the amazing life of Phyllis Schlafly.

Schweizer, Peter, *Do As I Say (Not as I Do)* (New York: Doubleday, 2005). Exposes contradictions between the public stances and personal conduct of prominent members of the loony left.

Skorski, Alan, *Pants on Fire: How Al Franken Lies, Smears, and Deceives* (Nashville: WND Books, 2005).

Smith, Mark. *Disrobed: The New Battle Plan to Break the Left's Stranglehold on the Courts* (New York: Three Rivers Press, 2006). My battle plan for reclaiming the courts.

Sowell, Thomas, *Black Rednecks and White Liberals* (New York: Encounter Books, 2005). Collection of essays showcasing the most enlightening results of Sowell's twenty-five years of fearless and groundbreaking research on racial and cultural issues.

Sowell, Thomas, *Controversial Essays* (Stanford, CA: Hoover Institution Press, 2002). If Sowell writes it, it's a must-read, and this book of essays is no exception.

Spencer, Robert, *Religion of Peace? Why Christianity Is and Islam Isn't* (Washington, D.C.: Regnery, 2007). The title says it all.

Steyn, Mark, *America Alone: The End of the World as We Know it* (Washington, D.C.: Regnery, 2006). Can a book be depressing and hilarious at the same time? Mark Steyn does it with this jeremiad arguing that Western civilization is doomed outside of America.

Stroup, Richard L., *Eco-nomics: What Everyone Should Know About Economics and the Environment* (Washington, D.C.: Cato Institute, 2003). Discusses free market environmentalism.

Tanner, Michael D., *The Poverty of Welfare: Helping Others in the Civil Society* (Washington, D.C.: Cato Institute, 2003). Criticizes government welfare and while discussing the role of private philanthropy and charity in combating poverty.

Weaver, Henry Grady, *The Mainspring of Human Progress* (Irvington, NY: The Foundation for Economic Education, 1997). Originally published in 1947, this was one of the first "conservative movement" books. It's an easy-to-read, common-sense volume discussing the role of business and technology in advancing human societies.

Will, George F., *With a Happy Eye But . . .: America and the World, 1997–2002* (New York: Free Press, 2002). Collection of writings by the acclaimed conservative columnist, including his analysis of the September 11 attacks.

Williams, Walter E., *Do the Right Thing* (Stanford, CA: Hoover Institution Press, 1995). Another must-read compilation.

Williams, Walter E., *More Liberty Means Less Government: Our Founders Knew This Well* (Stanford, CA: Hoover Institution Press, 1999). A compilation of must-read essays defending human liberty and criticizing government by one of America's most intelligent and lucid writers.

VRWC VOTING GUIDE

SENATE VOTE ON McCAIN-KENNEDY IMMIGRATION BILL CLOTURE

The following list shows the cloture vote on the McCain–Kennedy illegal immigrant amnesty bill. Those voting "yea" effectively voted to keep the amnesty bill alive, while those voting "nay" effectively voted to kill it.

YEAS – 46

Akaka (D-HI)
Bennett (R-UT)
Biden (D-DE)
Boxer (D-CA)
Cantwell (D-WA)
Cardin (D-MD)
Carper (D-DE)
Casey (D-PA)
Clinton (D-NY)
Conrad (D-ND)
Craig (R-ID)
Dodd (D-CT)
Durbin (D-IL)
Feingold (D-WI)
Feinstein (D-CA)
Graham (R-SC)

Gregg (R-NH)
Hagel (R-NE)
Inouye (D-HI)
Kennedy (D-MA)
Kerry (D-MA)
Klobuchar (D-MN)
Kohl (D-WI)
Kyl (R-AZ)
Lautenberg (D-NJ)
Leahy (D-VT)
Levin (D-MI)
Lieberman (ID-CT)
Lincoln (D-AR)
Lott (R-MS)
Lugar (R-IN)
Martinez (R-FL)

McCain (R-AZ)
Menendez (D-NJ)
Mikulski (D-MD)
Murray (D-WA)
Nelson (D-FL)
Obama (D-IL)
Reed (D-RI)
Reid (D-NV)
Salazar (D-CO)
Schumer (D-NY)
Snowe (R-ME)
Specter (R-PA)
Whitehouse (D-RI)
Wyden (D-OR)

NAYS – 53

Alexander (R-TN)
Allard (R-CO)
Barrasso (R-WY)
Baucus (D-MT)
Bayh (D-IN)
Bingaman (D-NM)
Bond (R-MO)
Brown (D-OH)
Brownback (R-KS)
Bunning (R-KY)
Burr (R-NC)
Byrd (D-WV)
Chambliss (R-GA)
Coburn (R-OK)
Cochran (R-MS)
Coleman (R-MN)
Collins (R-ME)
Corker (R-TN)

Cornyn (R-TX)
Crapo (R-ID)
DeMint (R-SC)
Dole (R-NC)
Domenici (R-NM)
Dorgan (D-ND)
Ensign (R-NV)
Enzi (R-WY)
Grassley (R-IA)
Harkin (D-IA)
Hatch (R-UT)
Hutchison (R-TX)
Inhofe (R-OK)
Isakson (R-GA)
Landrieu (D-LA)
McCaskill (D-MO)
McConnell (R-KY)
Murkowski (R-AK)

Nelson (D-NE)
Pryor (D-AR)
Roberts (R-KS)
Rockefeller (D-WV)
Sanders (I-VT)
Sessions (R-AL)
Shelby (R-AL)
Smith (R-OR)
Stabenow (D-MI)
Stevens (R-AK)
Sununu (R-NH)
Tester (D-MT)
Thune (R-SD)
Vitter (R-LA)
Voinovich (R-OH)
Warner (R-VA)
Webb (D-VA)

NOT VOTING – 1

Johnson (D-SD)

SUCCESSFUL SUPREME COURT APPOINTMENTS

President George W. Bush: John Roberts, Samuel Alito
President Bill Clinton: Ruth Bader Ginsberg, Stephen Breyer

Current total representation

Senate:

Democrats – 49
Republicans – 49
Independent Democrat – 1
Independent – 1

House of Representatives:

Democrats – 231
Republicans – 202
Vacant seats – 2

Key Senate Committee Chairmen:

Judiciary – Patrick Leahy (D-VT)
Homeland Security and Governmental Affairs – Joe Lieberman (ID-CT)
Health, Education, Labor, and Pensions – Ted Kennedy (D – MA)
Foreign Relations – Joseph Biden (D-DE)
Armed Services – Carl Levin (D-MI)
Budget – Kent Conrad (D-ND)
Finance – Max Baucus (D-MT)

Previous Senate Committee Chairmen, when Republicans Controlled the Senate:

Judiciary – Arlen Specter (R-PA)
Homeland Security and Governmental Affairs – Susan Collins (R-MA)
Health, Education, Labor, and Pensions – Michael Enzi (R-WY)
Foreign Relations – Dick Lugar (R-IN)
Armed Services – John Warner (R-VA)
Budget – Judd Greg (R-NH)
Finance – Charles Grassley (R-IA)

Key House Committee Chairman:

Judiciary – John Conyers, Jr. (D-MI)
Armed Services – Ike Skelton (D-MO)
Appropriations – David Obey (D-WI)
Foreign Affairs – Tom Lantos (D-CA)
Budget – John Spratt (D-SC)
Homeland Security – Bennie Thompson (D-MS)
Ways and Means – Charles Rangel (D-NY)

Previous House Committee Chairmen, when Republicans controlled the House:

Judiciary – Jim Sensenbrenner (R-WI)
Armed Services – Duncan Hunter (R-CA)
Appropriations – Jerry Lewis (R-CA)
Foreign Affairs – Henry Hyde (R-IL)
Budget – Jim Nussle (R-IA)
Homeland Security – Peter King (R-NY)
Ways and Means – Bill Thomas (R-CA)

Electoral College results since 1900

R   – Republican
D   – Democrat
D-P – Democrat-Populist
P   – Progressive

1900:   William McKinley [R] – 292
        William J. Bryan [D-P] – 155

1904:   Theodore Roosevelt [R] – 336
        Alton B. Parker [D] – 140

1908:   William H. Taft [R] – 321
        William J. Bryan [D] – 162

1912:   Woodrow Wilson [D] – 435
        Theodore Roosevelt [P] – 88

1916:   Woodrow Wilson [D] – 277
        Charles E. Hughes [R] – 254

1920:   Warren G. Harding [R] – 404
        James M. Cox [D] – 127

1924:   Calvin Coolidge [R] – 382
        John W. Davis [D] – 136

1928:   Herbert C. Hoover [R] – 444
        Alfred E. Smith [D] – 87

1932:   Franklin D. Roosevelt [D] – 472
         Herbert C. Hoover [R] – 59

1936:   Franklin D. Roosevelt [D] – 523
         Alfred M. Landon [R] – 8

1940:   Franklin D. Roosevelt [D] – 449
         Wendell L. Wilkie [R] – 82

1944:   Franklin D. Roosevelt [D] – 432
         Thomas E. Dewey [R] – 99

1948:   Harry S. Truman [D] – 303
         Thomas E. Dewey [R] – 189

1952:   Dwight D. Eisenhower [R] – 442
         Adlai Stevenson [D] – 89

1956:   Dwight D. Eisenhower [R] – 457
         Adlai Stevenson [D] – 73

1960:   John F. Kennedy [D] – 303
         Richard M. Nixon [R] – 219

1964:   Lyndon B. Johnson [D] – 486
         Barry M. Goldwater [R] – 52

1968:   Richard M. Nixon [R] – 301
         Hubert H. Humphrey [D] – 191

1972:   Richard M. Nixon [R] – 520
         George S. McGovern [D] – 17

1976:   Jimmy Carter [D] – 297
         Gerald R. Ford [R] – 240

1980:   Ronald Reagan [R] – 489
         Jimmy Carter [D] – 49

1984: Ronald Reagan [R] – 525
Walter F. Mondale [D] – 13

1988: George Bush [R] – 426
Michael S. Dukakis [D] – 111

1992: William J. Clinton [D] – 370
George Bush [R] – 168

1996: William J. Clinton [D] – 379
Bob Dole [R] – 159

2000: George W. Bush [R] – 271
Al Gore [D] – 267

2004: George W. Bush [R] – 286
John F. Kerry [D] – 251

Source: http://www.archives.gov/federal-register/electoral-college/scores.html#1900

ELECTION NIGHT SCORECARD

Total Needed to Win: 270

State	Electoral votes	Democrat/Republican Win
Alabama	9	
Alaska	3	
Arizona	10	
Arkansas	6	
California	55	
Colorado	9	
Connecticut	7	
Delaware	3	
DC	3	
Florida	27	
Georgia	15	
Hawaii	4	
Idaho	4	
Illinois	21	
Indiana	11	
Iowa	7	
Kansas	6	
Kentucky	8	
Louisiana	9	
Maine	4	
Maryland	10	
Massachusetts	12	

State	Electoral votes	Democrat/Republican Win
Michigan	17	
Minnesota	10	
Mississippi	6	
Missouri	11	
Montana	3	
Nebraska	5	
Nevada	5	
New Hampshire	4	
New Jersey	15	
New Mexico	5	
New York	31	
North Carolina	15	
North Dakota	3	
Ohio	20	
Oklahoma	7	
Oregon	7	
Pennsylvania	21	
Rhode Island	4	
South Carolina	8	
South Dakota	3	
Tennessee	11	
Texas	34	
Utah	5	
Vermont	3	
Virginia	13	
Washington	11	
West Virginia	5	
Wisconsin	10	
Wyoming	3	
Total	**538**	

NOTES

Chapter 1: Illegal Immigration: Killing Amnesty Until It's Dead

1   "Number of illegal immigrants hits 12m," Breitbart news service, http://www.breitbart.com/article.php?id=D8G6U2KO8&show_article=1.

2   "Immigration Strategies Taking Shape," *Houston Chronicle*, October 4, 2007.

3   "Bush Amnesty Sparks Surge in Border Crossings," FOXnews.com, February 19, 2004, http://www.foxnews.com/story/0,2933,111818,00.html.

4   "In Germany, Muslims Grow Apart," *International Herald Tribune*, December 4, 2005.

5   Http://corner.nationalreview.com/post/?q=NDQ3YTVmNGViZTk1ZTk0MzBmYz VlYml1ZDg1MDQ5NDc=.

6   "Effort to Curb Illegal Workers' Hiring Blocked," *Washington Post*, October 11, 2007.

7   "New Troops at U.S. Border, But the Task Is Vast," *Christian Science Monitor*, July 27, 2006.

8   Department of Homeland Security Fact Sheet, August 10, 2007, http://www .dhs.gov/xnews/releases/pr_1186757867585.shtm.

9   "Report Urges Troops Sent to Border," *Washington Times*, May 23, 2005.

10 This, according to Congressman Duncan Hunter. See his presidential campaign Web site, http://www.gohunter08.com/inner.asp?z=19.

11 "Border Fence Construction Not Moving Fast Enough for Rep. Hunter," *New York Times*, July 11, 2007.

12 Ibid.

13 "FBI's Mueller: Hezbollah busted in Mexican smuggling operation," Newsmax.com, March 30, 2006.

14 "Brothers Charged in Terror Plot Lived Illegally in U.S. for 23 years," FOXnews.com, May 9, 2007.

15 "Ahmed Ressam's millennium plot," PBS Frontline, http://www.pbs.org/wgbh/
    pages/frontline/shows/trail/inside/cron.html

16 Ann Coulter, "1 Down, 11,999,999 to Go," *Human Events Online*, August 22,
    2007, http://www.humanevents.com/article.php?id=22069.

17 Steve Sailer, "New Republican Majority?" *The American Conservative*, May 8,
    2006.

18 "Ethnic issues in California recall play out at Latino parade," *New York Times*,
    September 8, 2003, and "The California recall: the balloting; signaling voter
    unrest, Schwarzenegger cut deep into Democratic base," *New York Times*,
    October 9, 2003.

19 Nicholas Confessore, "Spitzer Drops Bid to Offer Licenses More Widely,"
    New York Times, November 19, 2007.

20 J. D. Hayworth, *Whatever It Takes* (Washington, D.C.: Regnery, 2005), 165.

21 See, for example, the photos at http://michellemalkin.com/2006/05/02/the-
    pictures-you-wont-see/.

22 Remarks by President Clinton at Portland State University Commencement,
    June 13, 1998, http://www.shusterman.com/prez.html.

23 Ibid.

24 Newt Gingrich, "Is the U.S. government out to undermine English?" Human
    Events Online, April 30, 2007, http://www.humanevents.com/article.php?id=
    20486.

25 Mickey Kaus, "Has the GOP found its 2006 issue?" http://slate.com/id/
    2138371/.

26 Dean E. Murphy, "Imagining Life Without Illegal Immigrants," *New York Times*,
    January 11, 2004, 1

27 Michael E. Fix and Karen Tumlin, "Welfare Reform and the Devolution of
    Immigrant Policy," The Urban Institute, New Federalism Issues and Options for
    States, October 1997.

28 U.S. State Department Country Report on Human Rights Practices, Mexico,
    2006, http://www.state.gov/g/drl/rls/hrrpt/2006/78898.htm.

Chapter 2: The War on Terror: Appease This!

1 "Fighting for the Enemy," National Review Online, http://article.nationalreview
   .com/?q=ZTRlNTA0Yzg0OTAyMWMwNzE4ZGJiODlhNzcxYTA2MmM=.

2 "Dead Taliban Leader was Training U.S. Recruits," ABC News, http://blogs.abcnews.com/theblotter/2007/05/dead_taliban_le.html.

3 Marc Sageman, "The Normality of Global Jihadi Terrorism," *The Journal of International Security Affairs*, Spring 2005, No. 8.

4 For an in-depth explanation of the Saudi role in disseminating the pro-terror Wahhabi ideology, see Dore Gold, *Hatred's Kingdom* (Washington, D.C.: Regnery, 2003).

5 Http://www.freedomhouse.org/template.cfm?page=138&report=45.

6 Http://www.rasmussenreports.com/public_content/politics/22_believe_ bush_knew_about_9_11_attacks_in_advance.

7 "Final Report on the Collapse of the World Trade Center Towers," National Institute of Standards and Technology, http://wtc.nist.gov/NISTNCSTAR1 CollapseofTowers.pdf.

8 "Debunking the 9/11 Myths," *Popular Mechanics*, March 2005.

9 "9/11 Conspiracies: Fact or Fiction," The History Channel.

10 "Profile: Mahnoud Ahmadinejad, Childhood Friends Offer Insight on Iran's Often Controversial President," ABC News, January 4, 2005, http://abcnews .go.com/wnt/story?id=1471465.

11 For photos, see http://littlegreenfootballs.com/weblog/?entry=19070&only and http://michellemalkin.com/2006/05/06/the-never-ending-cartoon-jihad/.

12 Karl Rove, "Remarks of Karl Rove at the New York Conservative Party," June 22, 2006, http://www.washingtonpost.com/wp-dyn/content/article/2005/06/24/ AR2005062400097.html.

Chapter 3: Federal Spending: In Your Face and Out of Control

1 Charles Schumer, "Big Government Looks Better Now," *Washington Post*, December 11, 2001.

2 Phil Kerpen, "The Federal Spend-A-Thon Continues," *National Review Online*, February 13, 2006.

3 Ibid.

4 "Farm Aid Plumps Up Iraq Funding," *USA Today*, March 22, 2007.

5 "President Bush Announces Five-Year, $30 Billion HIV/AIDS Plan," U.S. State Department, May 30, 2007, http://usinfo.state.gov/xarchives/display.html?p= washfile-english&y=2007&m=May&x=20070530161954lcnirellep0.4527094.

6   "Statement by Secretary John W. Snow," U.S. State Department, http://usinfo
    .state.gov/af/africa/aid_to_africa/nav_snow.html.

7   "Charitable Gifts Set New Record in 2006," *Houston Chronicle*, June 25, 2007,
    http://www.chron.com/disp/story.mpl/ap/fn/4917978.html.

8   "African corruption is a crime against humanity," *Christian Science Monitor*,
    August 9, 2004.

9   "220bn stolen by Nigeria's corrupt rulers," *Daily Telegraph*, June 26, 2005.
    http://www.telegraph.co.uk/news/main.jhtml?xml=/news/2005/06/25/wnig25.xml.

10 Transcript, *Meet the Press*, June 26, 2006, http://www.msnbc.msn.com/id/
    8332675/.

11 Linda Chavez, "D.C. Schools a Disgrace," February 5, 2003, http://www
    .townhall.com/columnists/LindaChavez/2003/02/05/dc_schools_a_disgrace.

12 Neal McCluskey, "A Lesson in Waste," Cato Institute, Policy Analysis, No. 518,
    July 7, 2004.

13 Dan Lips and Even Feinberg, "The Administrative Burden of No Child Left
    Behind," The Heritage Foundation, March 23, 2007.

14 Richard Vedder, "The Real Costs of Federal Aid to Higher Education," The
    Heritage Foundation, January 12, 2007.

15 "Timing of gifts stirs 'earmark' debate," *USA Today*, October 17, 2007.

16 Neal McCluskey, "A Lesson in Waste," Cato Institute, Policy Analysis, No. 518,
    July 7, 2004.

17 Stephen Moore, "Clear-Eyed Optimists," *Wall Street Journal*, October 5, 2007.

18 Robert E. Rector, Kirk A Johnson and Sarah E. Youssef, "The Extent of Material
    Hardship and Poverty in the United States," Heritage Foundation, http://www
    .heritage.org/Research/Welfare/wm187.cfm (originally published in *Review of
    Social Economy*, Fall 1999).

19 Robert Rector, "Welfare: Broadening the Reform," Heritage Foundation's
    Issues 2000 (2000), 293.

Chapter 4: The Courts: An Oligarchy in Robes

1   "Voters pass all eleven bans on gay marriage," MSNBC,
    http://www.msnbc.msn.com/id/6383353/

2   Data from Stateline.org, an independent element of the Pew Research Center,
    http://archive.stateline.org/flash-data/2007_May_31-CivilUnions/Social_Policy.pdf.

3   Mark Levin, *Men in Black* (Washington, D.C.: Regnery, 2005), 20–21.

4   Ibid., 19.

5   "Transcript of Discussion Between U.S. Supreme Court Justices Antonin Scalia
     and Stephen Breyer—AU Washington College of Law, Jan. 13," http://domino
     .american.edu/AU/media/mediarel.nsf/1D265343BDC2189785256B810071F238/
     1F2F7DC4757FD01E85256F890068E6E0?OpenDocument.

6   Scalia dissent, *Atkins v. Virginia*, 536 U.S. 304 (2002).

7   Thomas concurrence, *Foster v. Florida*, 537 U.S. 990 (2002).

8   "Transcript of Discussion Between U.S. Supreme Court Justices Antonin Scalia
     and Stephen Breyer—AU Washington College of Law, Jan. 13," http://domino
     .american.edu/AU/media/mediarel.nsf/1D265343BDC2189785256B810071F238/
     1F2F7DC4757FD01E85256F890068E6E0?OpenDocument.

9   Kevin R. C. Gutzman, *The Politically Incorrect Guide™ to the Constitution*
     (Washington, D.C.: Regnery, 2007), 177.

10   Mark Levine, *Men in Black* (Washington, D.C.: Regnery, 2005), 38.

11   "NOT made in China," *BusinessWeek*, July 30, 2007.

12   "Survey Says Personal Liability Limits Fail to Keep Pace with Growth in
     Household Assets," May 25, 2001, Jury Verdict Research data, http://www
     .insurancejournal.com/news/national/2001/05/25/14011.htm.

13   "Judge who seeks millions for lost pants has his (emotional) day in court,"
     Washington Post, June 13, 2007, and "Judge who filed suit plans to appeal
     defeat," *Washington Post*, August 15, 2007.

14   "Litigation Lottery costs America $865 billion per year," Pacific Research
     Institute, http://www.pacificresearch.org/publications/id.2853/pub_
     detail.asp.

15   Ibid.

16   Lott, *Freedomnomics*, 46.

17   "Medical Liability Reform—NOW!", *American Medical Association*, July 19,
     2006, http://www.ama-assn.org/ama1/pub/upload/mm/-1/mlrnow.pdf.

Chapter 5: Taxes: The Only Legal Form of Theft

1   Brian Riedl, "Tax Cut Myths and Realities," The Heritage Foundation, March 8,
     2007, http://www.heritage.org/Press/Commentary/ed031207b.cfm.

2   James Sherk, "Jobs, Taxes, and the Goldilocks Economy, The Heritage Foundation, February 1, 2007, http://www.heritage.org/Research/Economy/wm1336.cfm.

3   Brian Riedl, "Tax cut myths and realities," The Heritage Foundation, March 8, 2007, http://www.heritage.org/Press/Commentary/ed031207b.cfm.

4   White House Fact Sheet, http://www.whitehouse.gov/omb/pubpress/msr/msr_factsheet_071107.pdf.

5   "Bush Signs $350 Billion Tax Cut Measure; Some Americans Will Get Refunds in July; Payroll Deductions to Drop in June," Washington Post, May 29, 2003.

6   "Clinton's big tax hike," New York Sun, May 30, 2007.

7   "Edwards introduces plan for health care coverage," Washington Post, February 6, 2007.

8   "Taxes on wealthy would rise under Obama health care plan," Chicago Sun Times, May 29, 2007.

9   "Exxon profit hits record $39.5 billion," Los Angeles Times, February 2, 2007.

10 "Profit-snatching Sen. Clinton," Chattanooga Times Free Press, February 13, 2007.

11 These numbers as of 2005. See Jonathan Williams, "Local, State, and Federal Gas Taxes Consume 45.9 Cents Per Gallon on Average," Tax Foundation, September 13, 2005, http://www.taxfoundation.org/news/show/1054.html.

12 Chris Edwards, "Income tax rife with complexity and inefficiency," CATO Institute, http://www.cato.org/pubs/tbb/tbb-0604-33.pdf. "Wyden and Emanuel to Introduce 'Fair Flat Tax Act' Today," Tax Policy Blog, Tax Foundation, http://www.taxfoundation.org/blog/show/22338.html.

13 Steve Forbes, Flat Tax Revolution (Washington, D.C.: Regnery, 2005), 17.

14 Neal Boortz and John Linder, The FairTax Book (New York: ReganBooks, 2005).

15 Henry Hazlitt, Economics in One Lesson (New York: Three Rivers Press, 1988), 26.

16 Leonard E. Read, Anything That's Peaceful (Irvington, NY: Foundation for Economic Education, 1998), 10–11.

17 "Summary of Latest Federal Individual Income Tax Data," Tax Foundation, September 25, 2006, http://www.taxfoundation.org/taxdata/show/250.html.

18 All information courtesy of the Americans for Tax Reform Foundation.

19 "Ditto Democrats," Washington Post, September 21, 2007.

20 Rush Limbaugh, *The Way Things Ought To Be* (New York: Pocket Star, 1992), 78.

21 Read, *Anything That's Peaceful*, 44.

22 "Reluctant Class Warriors," *Wall Street Journal*, August 3, 2007.

23 Though I have heard this argument in the past, I was reminded of many of these points during a speech given by Grover Norquist of the Americans for Tax Reform Foundation, during a lecture in New York in October 2003. I have done my best to paraphrase his excellent presentation.

24 For good defenses of the Reagan economy, see Dinesh D'Souza, *Ronald Reagan: How an Ordinary Man Became an Extraordinary Leader*, and Peter B. Sperry, Ph.D., *The Real Reagan Economic Record: Responsible and Successful Fiscal Policy*.

Chapter 6: Intrusiveness of Government: Welcome to the Nanny State

1 John Lott, *Freedomnomics* (Washington, D.C.: Regnery, 2007), 68.

2 "John Edwards' universal health care plan would make regular checkups mandatory," FOXnews.com, September 3, 2007, http://www.foxnews.com/story/0,2933,295555,00.html.

3 " 'NHS should not treat those with unhealthy lifestyles' say Tories," Thisislondon.co.uk, September 4, 2007, http://www.thisislondon.co.uk/news/article-23410977-details/%27NHS+should+not+treat+those+with+unhealthy+lifestyles%27+say+Tories/article.do.

4 "Hill eyes national cigarette curb," *New York Post*, August 28, 2007.

5 "It's Official: Belmont Bans Smoking in Some Homes," NBC11.com, October 10, 2007, http://www.nbc11.com/news/14307719/detail.html.

6 John Stossel, "Stossel: Trans Fat Ban Is 'Nanny State' Intrusion," ABC News, December 6, 2006, http://abcnews.go.com/2020/story?id=2705411&page=1.

7 Chris Horner, *The Politically Incorrect Guide™ to Global Warming and Environmentalism* (Washington, D.C.: Regnery, 2007), 116.

8 Timothy Ball, "Global warming: The cold hard facts?" *Canada Free Press*, February 5, 2007, http://www.canadafreepress.com/2007/global-warming020507.htm.

9 Horner, 65–80.

10 "How global warming can chill the planet," *Live Science*, December 17, 2004, http://www.livescience.com/environment/041217_sealevel_rise.html.

11 "Steinmeier: climate change growing threat to peace," *Reuters*, October 23, 2007, http://www.reuters.com/article/latestCrisis/idUSL23331817.

12 "Who to scapegoat for the wildfires?" Scripps Howard News Service, October 24, 2007, and "Feds join probe in SoCal wildfire," *My Way News*, October 24, 2007, http://apnews.myway.com/article/20071025/D8SFUL0O0.html.

13 "Game over on global warming?" *Los Angeles Times*, February 5, 2007.

14 Ibid.

15 "Having large families 'is an eco-crime,'" *Sunday Times*, May 6, 2007.

16 http://www.huffingtonpost.com/sheryl-crow/laurie-and-sheryl-go-to-s_b_ 46320.html.

17 "Keeping Them Honest: The Truth about Global Warming," CNN transcript, October 19, 2007, http://transcripts.cnn.com/TRANSCRIPTS/0710/19/se.01 .html.

18 George Will, "The Media and Global Warming," Townhall.com, April 12, 2007.

19 Philip Howard, *Death of Common Sense: How Law Is Suffocating America* (New York: Warner Books, 1996), 14.

20 Jonathan Klick and Thomas Stratman, "First, Do No Harm," *Regulation*, Spring 2003, 9; Jonathan Klick and Thomas Stratman, "Offsetting Behavior in the Workplace," April 14, 2003.

21 Ibid.

22 Tammy O. Tengs, "Optimizing Societal Investments in the Prevention of Premature Death," doctoral dissertation, School of Public Health, Harvard University, June 1994.

23 Erin M. Hymel and Lawrence W. Whitman, "Regulation: Reining in the Federal Bureaucracy," The Heritage Foundation research paper (citing Kenneth Cole, "Federal Rules Fuel the Size Gap between Trucks and Cars," *Detroit News*, March 29, 1998). See also Julie Defalco, "The Deadly Effects of Fuel Economy Standards: CAFE's Lethal Impact on Auto Safety," June 1999, http://www.cei .org/pdf/1631.pdf.

24 Hymel and Whitman, "Regulation: Reining in the Federal Bureaucracy."

25 Ibid.

26 Angela Antonelli, Heritage Foundation, *Regulation*, 1998 Candidate's Book, Chapter 3. See also Christopher Douglass, Michael Orlando, and Melinda Warren, "Regulatory Changes and Trends: An Analysis of the 1998 Budget of

the United States Government," *Policy Brief* No. 182, Center for the Study of American Business, August 1997, and James Gattuso, "What is the Bush Administration's Record on Regulatory Reform?" The Heritage Foundation, November 17, 2004, http://www.heritage.org/Research/HomelandSecurity/tst111604a.cfm#_ftnref1.

27 Randall Fitzgerald, *Mugged by the State: Outrageous Government Assaults on Ordinary People and their Property* (Washington, D.C.: Regnery 2003).

28 The Congressional Review Act (CRA), Subtitle E of Title II (Small Business Regulatory Enforcement Fairness Act) of the Contract With America Advancement Act of 1996, established an expedited process by which Congress reviews and may disapprove any final federal agency regulation. See also Thomas Hopkins, "Regulatory Costs in Profile," *Policy Study* No. 132, Center for the Study of American Business, August 1996.

29 Statement of Scott Moody, Senior Economist, Tax Foundation, "The Cost of Tax Compliance," before the Subcommittee on Oversight of the Ways and Means Committee of the U.S. House of Representatives, July 17, 2001.

30 Economist Joseph Schumpeter is often credited with coining the idea of "creative destruction" in the 1940s.

Chapter 7: The Iraq War: Surrender Is Not a Winning Strategy

1 "Iran's secret plan for summer offensive to force US out of Iraq," *The Guardian*, May 22, 2007.

2 Http://edition.cnn.com/TRANSCRIPTS/0511/30/se.01.html.

3 "Setting the Record Straight: Democrats On An Artificial Timetable In Iraq," White House document, http://www.whitehouse.gov/news/releases/2005/11/20051130-9.html.

4 Joseph Farah, "Between the lines: a big problem for Democrats," Human Events Online, August 8, 2007, http://www.humanevents.com/article.php?id=21870#continueA.

5 "Stark's comments on war incite GOP backlash," MSNBC.com, October 19, 2007, http://www.msnbc.msn.com/id/21375855.

6 Http://michellemalkin.com/2007/10/18/stark-raving-mad/.

7 Anne Bayefsky, "Our dead are our fault," National Review Online, September 28, 2007, http://article.nationalreview.com/?q=MzBlNTU5MTgzYmQ2NGQ2Njc4ZmMxMDVmZDU3ZWM5MGQ.

8   "President William J. Clinton, Address to the Nation on the Bombing of Iraq," December 16, 1998.

Chapter 8: Social Security and Other Entitlements: Our Failed Experiment in Socialism

1   "Is Social Security in Trouble," *Heritage Forum*, Vol 1, No 1, 6.

2   "Remarks by Ben Bernanke to the Washington Economic Club, October 4, 2006," http://www.federalreserve.gov/boardDocs/speeches/2006/20061004/default.htm.

3   "Obama Floats Social Security Tax Hike," ABC News, September 22, 2007, http://abcnews.go.com/Politics/Story?id=3638710&page=1.

4   "Is Social Security in Trouble," *Heritage Forum*, 6, 8.

5   "Obama Floats Social Security Tax Hike," ABC News, September 22, 2007, http://abcnews.go.com/Politics/Story?id=3638710&page=1.

6   Ibid., 6, 11.

7   Ibid., 20.

8   "Tax Cuts Re-Examined," *Washington Post*, August 15, 2004.

9   Mark Steyn, "Tough Days for Freedom," National Review Online, September 23, 2007, http://article.nationalreview.com/?q=MTdmZDUxOTIzNDhjNzQyNDBiMWRmZTFhYTQyNjNiNzU=.

10 Cato Handbook on Policy, 6th Edition (2005), Cato Institute, http://www.cato.org/pubs/handbook/hb109/hb_109-8.pdf.

11 John Lott, *Freedomnomics* (Washington, D.C.: Regnery, 2007), 12.

12 Cato Handbook on Policy, 6th Edition (2005), Cato Institute, http://www.cato.org/pubs/handbook/hb109/hb_109-8.pdf.

13 "Projections Show Troubles Still Loom for Benefit Plans," *New York Times*, April 24, 2007.

14 Cato Handbook on Policy, 6th Edition (2005), Cato Institute, http://www.cato.org/pubs/handbook/hb109/hb_109-8.pdf.

15 "Success of Drug Plan Challenges Democrats," *Washington Post*, November 26, 2006.

16 "Projections Show Troubles Still Loom for Benefit Plans," *New York Times*, April 24, 2007.

17 Christine Kim and Robert Rector, "Welfare reform turns ten: Evidence shows reduced dependence, poverty," The Heritage Foundation, August 1, 2006, http://www.heritage.org/Research/Welfare/wm1183.cfm.

18 Ibid.

19 Stephen Moore and Julian Simon, *It's Getting Better All the Time* (Washington, D.C.: Cato Institute, 2000), 6.

20 Robert Rector, "How Poor Are America's Poor? Examining the 'Plague' of Poverty in America," The Heritage Foundation, August 27, 2007, http://www. heritage.org/Research/Welfare/bg2064.cfm.

21 Ibid.

Chapter 9: Abortion: Why Life Is the Right Choice

1 Ronald Reagan, *Abortion and the Conscience of the Nation* (Sacramento: New Regency Publishing, 2000), 39.

2 "Facts on Induced Abortion in the United States," Guttmacher Institute, May 2006, http://www.guttmacher.org/pubs/fb_induced_abortion.html.

3 "H-5.982 Late-Term Pregnancy Termination Techniques," American Medical Association, http://www.ama-assn.org/apps/pf_new/pf_online?f_n=browse& doc=policyfiles/HnE/H-5.982.HTM.

4 Ramesh Ponnuru, *Party of Death* (Washington, D.C.: Regnery, 2006), 47–48.

5 Ponnuru, *Party of Death*, 57.

6 Tammy Bruce, *The New American Revolution* (New York: William Morrow, 2005), 186.

7 John Lott, *Freedomnomics* (Washington, D.C.: Regnery, 2007), 121.

8 "Oops-onomics," *The Economist*, December 1, 2005.

9 Lott, *Freedomnomics*, 125. See pp. 117–127 for a thorough debunking of *Freakonomics*' abortion argument.

10 Reagan, *Abortion and the Conscience of the Nation*, 42.

11 William F. Buckley, Jr., "The Eternal Problem in Abortion Debate," *National Review*, June 16, 1997.

12 "Facts on Induced Abortion in the United States," Guttmacher Institute, May 2006, http://www.guttmacher.org/pubs/fb_induced_abortion.html.

13 American Life League, http://www.all.org/article.php?id=10229&search= "The%20life%20of%20a%20human%20being%20starts%20at%20fertilization, %20when%20the%20father's%20sperm%20unites%20with%20the%20mother's %20egg."

14 Moffit, et al., "Crime," 234.

15 Robert E. Moffit, et al., "Crime: Turning the Tide in America," *Issues '98: The Candidate's Briefing Book* (Washington, D.C.: Heritage Foundation),1998, 234.

Chapter 10: Media Bias: All the News That Fits the Slant

1   Http://radioequalizer.blogspot.com/2007/01/stephen-green-mark-green-air-america.html.

2   "Feminists' Hot Air," *New York Post*, April 20, 2007, and "Women's Fib?" *New York Post*, April 15, 2007.

3   "The Structural Imbalance of Political Talk Radio," Center for American Progress, http://www.americanprogress.org/issues/2007/06/pdf/talk_radio.pdf.

4   Eric Alterman, "Point, Counterpoint: The Conservative Beat," *The Nation*, December 25, 2006.

5   Ann Coulter, *Slander: Liberal Lies about the American Right* (New York: Three Rivers Press, 2002), 67.

6   "Correcting the Record; *Times* Reporter Who Resigned Leaves Long Trail of Deception," *New York Times*, May 11, 2003.

7   "Editor of *Times* Tell Staff He Accepts Blame for Fraud," *New York Times*, May 15, 2003.

8   "Mismanaging Diversity," *New York Post*, May 18, 2003.

9   Ibid.

10 " 'Get Smart' in Washington," editorial, *Wall Street Journal*, August 3, 2007.

11 "The Fear of Fear Itself," *New York Times*, August 7, 2007.

12 "Betraying Its Own Best Interests," *New York Times*, September 23, 2007.

13 See, for example, "When Peer Pressure, Not a Conscience, Is Your Guide," *New York Times*, March 31, 2006.

14 Ibid.

15 Stuart Taylor, speech to Cato Institute, September 11, 2007, Http://www.cato .org/event.php?eventid=4024. Taylor, along with KC Johnson, is the author of

Until Proven Innocent: Political Correctness and the Shameful Injustices of the Duke Lacrosse Rape Case (New York: Thomas Dunne Books, 2007).

16 "Files From Duke Rape Case Give Details but No Answers," *New York Times*, August 25, 2006.

17 "Revisiting the Times's Coverage of the Duke Rape Case," *New York Times*, April 22, 2007.

18 "Final Days," editorial, *Washington Post*, March 17, 2003.

19 "President Bush Prepares for War," editorial, *New York Times*, March 17, 2003.

20 Philip Bennett, "The Press: Too Far From the Story?" *Washington Post*, June 6, 2004.

21 "Military reporters and editors luncheon address in Washington D.C.," http://www.militaryreporters.org/sanchez_101207.html.

22 "Former top general in Iraq faults Bush administration," *New York Times*, October 12, 2007.

23 Http://blog.seattletimes.nwsource.com/davidpostman/archives/2007/08/a_newsroom_reprimand_at_the_times.html.

24 Eric Johnson, "The Untouchable Chief of Baghdad," Foundation for Defense of Democracies, June 29, 2004, http://www.defenddemocracy.org/research_topics/research_topics_show.htm?doc_id=231243.

25 John Heilemann, "The Truth, the Whole Truth, and Nothing But the Truth," *Wired*, November 2000, 264.

26 "Journalists dole out cash to politicians (quietly)," MSNBC.com, http://www.msnbc.msn.com/id/19113485/

27 Bill Sammon, *At Any Cost* (Washington, DC: Regnery, 2001), 41.

28 Ann Coulter, *Slander* (Three Rivers 2002), 109.

29 "What Went Wrong?" PBS website, November 5, 2004, http://www.pbs.org/newshour/bb/politics/july-dec04/exitpolls_11-05.html.

30 Wayne LaPierre and James Jay Baker, *Shooting Straight: Telling the Truth about Guns in America* (Washington, D.C.: Regnery, 2002), 22.

31 John R. Lott, Jr., *The Bias Against Guns* (Washington, D.C.: Regnery, 2003), 40.

32 "Recent Study On Media Bias Shows Need For Gun Owners To Speak Out," NRA Web site, http://www.nraila.org/Legislation/Federal/Read.aspx?id=3220.

BIG DISCOUNTS ON EXTRA COPIES
Help Keep the Conspiracy Going Strong!

Please consider ordering extra copies at bulk discounts for friends, business and social associates, local political groups, radio talk-show hosts, and newspaper editors.

To order multiple copies of *The Official Handbook of the Vast Right-Wing Conspiracy*, consult the discount schedule below and call 202-216-0601, ext. 430.

Special Bulk Copy Discount Schedule	
10–24 copies	20% OFF!
25-49 copies	35% OFF!
50-99 copies	40% OFF!
100-199 copies	45% OFF!
200 or more…	Call

Since 1947
REGNERY PUBLISHING, INC.
An Eagle Publishing Company • Washington, DC

CALL NOW: **202-216-0601** ext. **430**